Margaret Sanger sacrificed her marriage, family life, and health to educating women about contraception. Jailed nine times for defying blue laws, she managed to turn public opinion in her favor through pamphlets, speeches, clinics, and research. In her own lifetime, Mrs. Sanger finally saw the free dissemination of information that had been forbidden during her youth.

WOMEN OF AMERICA, a series of biographical works of which this book is a part, is under the general editorship of Milton Meltzer. Also in this series is *Sea and Earth: The Life of Rachel Carson.*

LAWRENCE LADER was a friend of Margaret Sanger, and the author of the first adult biography of her. MILTON MELTZER is the author of many biographies for young readers. Together they have written a moving account of a gentle person who fought to enrich the lives of women all over the world.

THE LAUREL-L~~~~~~~~~~~~~~~~~~~~~~~~~~der a single impr~~~~~~~~~~~~~~~~~~~~~~~~nd nonfiction pa~~~~~~~~~~~~~~~~~~~~~~~~ult readers, both ~~~~~~~~~~~~~~~~~~~~~~~~his series is unde~~~~~~~~~~~~~~~~~~~~~~~~ss, Distinguished ~~~~~~~~~~~~~~~~~~~~~~~~~, *jer*sey City State College, and Charles F. Reasoner, Professor of Elementary Education, New York University.

MARGARET SANGER

Pioneer of Birth Control

❧«»❧

LAWRENCE LADER
MILTON MELTZER

For our daughters—Amy, Jane, and Wendy

Published by
Dell Publishing Co., Inc.
1 Dag Hammarskjold Plaza
New York, New York 10017

Laurel-Leaf Library ® TM 766734, Dell Publishing Co., Inc.
Reprinted by arrangement with Thomas Y. Crowell Company
Printed in the United States of America
First Laurel printing—May 1974

Preface

The right of a woman to plan her family through birth control is one of the most crucial ideas of this century.

Today the right to practice birth control by "pill" or other medically approved methods has been established by the United States Supreme Court. It is so accepted by society that it seems hard to believe that Margaret Sanger went to jail nine times to win this right.

She was a unique crusader. She was not the hatchet-faced feminist newspaper cartoonists loved to ridicule, but a beautiful woman—gentle, almost shy, with a voice like liquid silver.

Her crusade against almost insurmountable odds affected the very roots of life—the quality and happiness both of marriage and of children. Margaret Sanger made it her basic principle that every child brought into the world must be wanted and loved, and given education and opportunity.

Through birth control Margaret Sanger saw the one hope of bringing reason and planning into family life, so that men and women would have only the number of children they wanted, when they wanted. To Margaret Sanger, birth control was the first freedom for women. "No woman can call herself free until she can choose consciously whether she will or will not be a mother," she wrote.

It was a revolutionary idea.

Contents

Acknowledgments

It was the good fortune of one of the authors, Lawrence Lader, to have the opportunity of hundreds of hours of interviews with the late Margaret Sanger during the writing of his earlier biography *The Margaret Sanger Story and the Fight for Birth Control,* published in 1955, and also to talk with scores of her friends and associates. Many of these, now dead, knew her from the earliest days of the birth control movement and thus offered a rare source of personal anecdote and reminiscence.

For that book, Mrs. Sanger also made available her personal papers and the two most important collections of material on her life and the movement—one in the Library of Congress, the other in the Smith College Library. The two collections together contain not only the most complete file of printed material from the birth of the movement, but also invaluable memoranda and correspondence with key personalities in Mrs. Sanger's intimate circle.

Smaller but valuable collections of material are at Planned Parenthood—World Population and the Margaret Sanger Research Bureau in New York City.

In writing this account of Margaret Sanger's life, the authors have, of course, made extensive use of the research that went into the earlier book, but it is otherwise completely new.

1. A HOUSEFUL OF HIGGINSES

There was nothing special about being born into the Higgins family. By the time Margaret came along, there had been five babies before her. Like all the others, she was brought into the world by her father, Michael Higgins. He was the only "doctor" the family ever had. And almost from infancy, Margaret helped in the delivery of every new brother and sister. When the eleventh and last little Higgins was born, sex and birth were no mystery to Margaret.

She was a strikingly pretty girl with wide-set gray eyes, and two braids of auburn hair that bounced rakishly off her shoulders. Gay and lively, with a flair for acting, she was often invited on

weekends to play with the children of the leading
citizens who lived on the hill above the river.

Corning, New York—where she was born in
1879—was a small factory center of less than ten
thousand people. The big glass works that had
yet to make its reputation lined the banks of the
Chemung River. Factory chimneys, jutting a hundred feet into the sky, poured dense gray smoke
over the homes of the workers below.

Up on the hill it was different. In the summer
ladies and gentlemen, relaxed in wicker chairs,
chatted quietly on the cool verandas. Soft green
lawns, interrupted here and there by tennis courts,
stretched down to the tree-lined streets. There
was a gulf between Irish worker and Yankee up-
per class, but Margaret was welcomed by parents who liked to see their children entertained
by her fairy tales or dramatic monologues. She
could invent games and make up stories, acting
out all the parts herself and keeping the children
laughing for hours.

Down below, her own life was lived in a small
house in a pine woods on the edge of town. The
Higgins family had moved from the center of
Corning when Margaret was a little girl. The
crowded riverbank was no place for her sick
mother. The families there—most of them recently from Ireland—huddled together in boxlike
houses. There were always too many children to
be clothed and fed, too many to care for, too
many to educate, on the small wages fathers
brought home.

Margaret soon noticed the difference between

these homes and those on the hill. Up there she rarely saw families with more than two or three children. Their mothers had time to play with them on the rolling lawn, or walk with them through the quiet streets. Their mothers looked fresh and pretty even when they reached the age of forty, while the mothers of the poor were worn out by the time they were thirty.

To improve his wife's health, Michael Higgins had moved his family out to the pine woods and the cleaner air. He had married Anne Purcell not just because she was Irish, too, but because she was slender and lovely, with gray-green eyes, wavy black hair, and a perfect skin. But the babies came one after the other. (Margaret always remembered her mother as pregnant or nursing a new baby.) The constant cooking and washing and cleaning and sewing and nursing drained her strength away. There was never a moment for herself, never time for a walk with her husband, or a concert or a play.

Now she coughed constantly, racking coughs so deep she had to lean against the wall to support herself. Everyone in the house would be still, ears strained, till the sound of the coughing subsided. "Consumption" they called it, the popular name for tuberculosis, a disease often linked to poverty.

Irish-born, Michael Hennessey Higgins had crossed the Atlantic as a boy with his family. At President Lincoln's first call for volunteers he had run away from home to join the Army. At seventeen he was a drummer in a New York cavalry regiment. When the war ended, he studied medicine, not to become a doctor, but because he wanted to be a sculptor. A knowledge of anatomy would help him perfect his skill in modeling the human body. He settled down in Corning to make his living chiseling out of marble and granite, angels and saints to adorn the local cemeteries.

It was not an easy way to earn a living. Work was irregular, and the fees never large enough to support so big a family in comfort. There was rarely money for extras or an unexpected treat. Christmas was the time Margaret waited for to get the pair of shoes she needed. Necessities might be all Michael Higgins could afford, but it did not shrivel his generous nature. Once he started out to get a dozen bananas for supper, but bought a stalk of fifteen dozen instead and gave them all to children he passed at play on his way home. Another time he showed up with the eight children of a neighbor in trouble and crowded them into the Higginses' household for months.

His bigheartedness showed best the day he invited Henry George, one of the leading radical thinkers of the time, to address a banquet in the main hotel. Although household bills were overdue and coal was needed for the winter, Higgins used his money to pay the cost of dinner for fifty guests. It was a splurge that tried Anne Higgins' patience severely.

But nothing like that could shake their marriage. Between them there was love, and more, there was a deep respect and comradeship that extended to the children as well. None of them was ever forced to take sides. Margaret knew that if she pleased her father, she pleased her mother equally. The children were rarely scolded and never spanked. When they had to be corrected, they were not humiliated in front of the others, but taken aside and talked to as adults.

Hard times never weakened Anne Higgins' love for her husband. Standing nearly six feet tall, with brilliant blue eyes, freckled skin, and a red mane of hair cresting a massive head, Michael Higgins looked like one of his own heroic statues. He reigned supreme over the family. He had a sculptor's strength and a good physician's tenderness. He nursed his wife through six weeks of pneumonia—a disease that in those days was often fatal—set broken legs, brought Margaret through a siege of typhoid fever. His basic medicine, in an era when doctors had scarcely any useful drugs, was "good whiskey." When Margaret's face was swollen with ivy poisoning, a doctor advised Higgins to paint it with iodine three times a day. The treatment was more agonizing than the illness, and her father switched back to whiskey. Margaret soon recovered.

2. BREAKING FREE

Corning was not the West, but Margaret grew up
under discipline such as the frontier demanded.
The Higgins children were trained to do every
task the household required. They could make
their own clothing, cook, sew, shingle a roof, milk
a cow, deliver a baby. Each child tended his own
patch of garden. Their father made all the furniture in the house. It was a simple life, a life
shared to the fullest. Margaret remembered later
the pride she felt in helping to carry all the responsibilities of the family.

What made the Higginses' household different
from others was the excitement over ideas that
crackled in the air. Michael Higgins was Corn-

ing's local rebel. He fought for free libraries, free education, free books in the public schools. His workshop was always full of friends—cabinet-maker, cobbler, mason, doctor, local editor—the townsfolk who did a little thinking for themselves. They loved to argue. Higgins' rich brogue would rise above the other voices, driving an opponent into a corner, while Margaret sat by in delight.

Little money or none, books were a necessity to her father, and his small library was one of the best in Corning. Margaret, too, became a hungry reader no end of books could satisfy. Higgins valued his beliefs, but he expected his children to have their own ideas. And he urged them to speak out. Learning and thinking were not something that went on only in school—if, indeed, they happened there at all. Their father's example was a daily reminder of the joy to be found in using your mind, in stretching it to its full power. He seemed drawn to every new idea, examining it for its worth no matter what others said against it. Equality of the sexes and the right of women to vote, ideas ridiculed by many, he stoutly defended.

But it was politics and economics that above all concerned him. How men made their living and how they organized their lives together were the heart of the matter. He became a Socialist because he considered socialism Christian belief put into daily practice. "Take care of yourself, no matter what may become of your fellow man," was the ethic of the wild beast, he said. Cain said unto the Lord, "Am I my brother's keeper?" Michael Higgins answering yes turned to ideas about a new social system that would make true brotherhood possible.

He loved to read from his books to his children, roaring with pleasure every time he found a pungent line. He made the children reread them "to elevate the mind."

"The one thing I've been able to give you is a free mind," he told Margaret. "Use it well and give something back to your generation."

Higgins was a freethinker, joining no church or religious group. But he urged his children to attend a different church every Sunday and to learn from each. "Try them all," he said to Margaret, "but be chained to none. You'll grow up when you begin to do your own thinking."

Anne Higgins had been born a Roman Catholic and had always attended church. But after her marriage, her husband's opposition to all formal religion gradually separated her from her early faith. Father Coghlan often called on her to send her children to parochial school, but Higgins would not permit it.

The final break with the church came when Higgins invited Colonel Robert Ingersoll, one of the noted freethinkers of his day, to address a meeting at Corning. Higgins had already paid the rent for the hall, which happened to be owned by the Catholic church. But when he and his friends arrived for the meeting, the doors were bolted. Father Coghlan had decided that Ingersoll's ideas were "too dangerous" to be given a hearing.

Mr. Higgins had taken ten-year-old Margaret with him to hear Colonel Bob. Now they stood together on the steps of the hall, facing a crowd yelling curses at Higgins and Ingersoll. Fighting broke out. Higgins tried to calm his fellow townsmen, but in a moment tomatoes and cabbages rained down on his head. Unshaken, he announced that he would not call off the meeting. He invited those who wanted to hear Ingersoll to walk to a clearing in the woods nearby. Holding Margaret's hand, he pushed through the throng, leading his small band of followers to the woods. There, standing on a tree stump, his red hair flaming against the setting sun, he introduced Ingersoll to the handful who had not been frightened off by the mob. The girl trembled in excitement as she listened to her father and Colonel Bob. She did not understand all they said, but she knew that for the sake of an idea, they had faced down a crowd's anger. She, too, would fight for her ideas when the time came.

For his defiance of the church, Michael Higgins was made to suffer. Much of his work had been for the local Roman Catholic cemeteries. His commissions had been shrinking in the past few years, but now they were completely cut off. He had to travel farther and farther from Corning to get work. He was gone for weeks sometimes, hating to be away from his family. But it was even worse when long months passed without any work. The ever present burden of debts grew heavier and heavier.

In the eyes of her schoolmates, Margaret, too,
was a rebel against the church. From that time on
she and all the Higgins children were known as
children of the devil. They were taunted by their
classmates, names were shouted at them in the
streets. It could not have been easy to suffer.
What helped was her own slowly growing sense
of the limitations of Corning itself. It was no
longer a place whose approval she had to have.
She did not care about boys who were interested
in little more than hunting and dogs, in girls who
talked only of party dresses and dates. She turned
inward, beginning to explore what she called
"the other me"—the Margaret who burned for
action and adventure, for romance and daring.
The women in the world around her led narrow
lives, she thought. Petty limits shut them in; social rules choked them; the need to please stunted
them. She felt a powerful desire to act, to do
something bold and brave, to test herself against
danger.

She began to set dares for herself. First she
went upstairs alone to bed without a light—
something she had dreaded from early childhood.
Then she went down into the dark cellar without
singing loudly as she always used to do. Then
she climbed high into the rafters of the barn and
leaped down into the hay stacked thirty feet below.

Now she thought she was ready for the hardest
test of all. On a farm across the river Margaret
had friends whose apples she loved. To get there

she walked three miles, taking a roundabout way across a sturdy wooden bridge. A far shorter route was to go by the nearby railroad bridge, suspended high over the river. But the one thing she feared most was to walk across its ties. There was always the danger of falling between the ties or even meeting a train as you crossed.

This day she resolved she would cross by that bridge. Her legs trembled as she neared it. But the more scared she felt, the more determined she was to overcome her fear. She started over slowly, setting her feet carefully on each tie. A quarter of the way across she heard the singing of the rails and knew a train was speeding toward her, hidden by a curve beyond the bridge. Then suddenly it was roaring down on her, a huge engine of death whose black smoke scarred the sky. She leaped to the side, trying to hide behind an iron girder. Her foot slipped, and she dropped—saved only because both arms could not pass through the crossbars. Her eyes shut tight, she hung in space, praying the engineer would not release scalding steam. She never knew how long she hung there. Then there was the sound of feet pounding over the ties, and arms were around her shoulders, pulling her back up to safety. It was a friend of her father's, fishing from the bridge, who had rescued her. He scolded her angrily and ordered her to go straight home.

But she knew she could never go home defeated. To return now would have been as impossible for her as to stop breathing. Frightened, bruised, bleeding, she still somehow completed the crossing. "After that I felt almost grown up," she wrote later. "I did not talk about it, but something inside me had conquered something else." She had proved she had the will and strength to make changes even in herself.

It was not long afterward that she showed her rebellion in school. It happened when she was finishing the eighth grade. A trivial thing was the cause of it. She was wearing a new pair of gloves to school that day, her first new pair which some-one had given her. She lingered a moment out-side, stretching them over her hands, admiring their look. When she came into the classroom a few minutes late, the teacher, a sour-tongued shrew, snapped at her: "So your ladyship has ar-rived." The class laughed. Margaret sat down and began to work at her books. But the teacher con-tinued to taunt her. Suddenly Margaret stood up, walked out of the school, went home, and an-nounced she would never go back again. She'd go to work, starve, die, but nothing on earth would make her change her mind.

A family council was called. They pleaded, begged, threatened. Did she think her education was complete? How would she earn a living? Did she want to bury herself in a factory? It ended when her older sisters, Mary and Nan, who were working now at tutoring and translating, decided that Margaret had the mind and will to profit from an advanced private school. They agreed on the Hudson River Institute at Claverack, a town about a hundred miles north of New York City. Mary and Nan would pool their funds to pay for her tuition and clothes, while Margaret would wash dishes and wait on table for her room and board.

She had broken free from Corning.

3. RINGLEADER

From her tight family unit in Corning, Margaret was suddenly transplanted into a home with five hundred boys and girls. The boys' rooms were at one end of a big building, and the girls' at the other. They all ate together, went to class together, and shared the athletic fields. (Coeducation, still not very common, had started early here.) For the first time Margaret met teachers who did not act like policemen. They were warm friends whose greater education and experience helped guide minds exploring the world of ideas.

There was more than small-town talk to feed on here. There were spirited girls who wore New

York fashions and discussed the latest books and plays. They were not snobs; although Margaret worked her way through school, she was always treated as an equal. She could speak her mind here—often echoing her father's opinions—and find herself admired for her boldness and her "advanced" ideas.

She was delighted to find going to school chapel no dry ritual. It was a platform for debate. On Saturday mornings the students in turn discussed social or political issues. Margaret wrote to her father, asking for background material on famous women of history, especially the rebels like the English Mary Wollstonecraft, the first outright feminist.

She wrote out her first speech, then stole away to the open fields to practice it again and again. Soon word got out that she would speak on "Women's Rights." Thinking it a big joke—as most men of the time did—the boys ridiculed Margaret; they drew cartoons of her wearing trousers and puffing on fat cigars.

Being made fun of did not stop her. She was already dreaming of herself as a new voice for women. Where most students dreaded speechmaking, she eagerly hunted down new subjects. She backed William Jennings Bryan and the radical Populists in the 1896 election, although she stood alone against the whole school. She thought she saw Utopia in the skies, she said, and wanted to take hold of it and plant it here on earth.

The depth of her feeling and the pleasure she

took in her ideas moved the audiences who heard
her in chapel. The elocution teacher encouraged
her to try poetry readings and acting. One day
Margaret thought, Why not a career on the stage?
Her sister Mary had taken her to see the famous
Maude Adams play Shakespeare's Juliet. And
Margaret, with the same rich auburn hair, be-
gan to dream of herself as another Maude Adams.
When she went home on vacation, she announced
to the family that she was going into the theater.

Michael Higgins laughed at the idea. But Mary
encouraged her and suggested she try to enter
one of the best dramatic schools in New York.
Back came the application blank with all the
usual formalities of age, height, color of eyes and
hair, and photos to be submitted.

But the application also demanded exact length
of leg as well as measurements of ankle, calf,
knee, thigh, bosom, hips. Margaret was startled.
She had expected to be judged by her ability to
act, speak, sing, dance, and by her personality.
What could such details of anatomy have to do
with being a second Maude Adams? Angrily she
tore up the application and decided to concentrate on work where more things counted than
the shape of her leg.

Some of the girls had warned Margaret that if
she kept voicing wild or radical views all the
time she would never get a man. But the boys
could not resist her vivid looks, her charm, her
qualities as a natural leader whether for a class
picnic, a choral group, or an escapade.

Toward the end of her last year at Claverack she proposed the idea that some of the girls should slip out of the dormitory window and meet their dates at the village dance hall. They got away safely and had been dancing for hours when Professor Flack, the headmaster, entered the hall. They were marched back to the school in ominous silence.

The next morning Margaret was summoned to Flack's office. "Miss Higgins," he said, "don't you feel ashamed for getting the girls into trouble last night? Because of you, they have broken the rules."

She thought at once that someone had told on her. But the headmaster went on, "No one had to tell me you were the ringleader. Again and again I've noticed your influence on the others. This leadership you have is a rare gift, Margaret. I want you to think about it in the future. You'll have to make a choice. You can use it to get yourself and others into trouble, or you can use it for constructive work which will benefit everyone."

That was all. There was no punishment. Instead she had wisely been made to think about this strength she felt inside her. Now she knew she had to learn to shape it to some purpose.

When her three years at Claverack ended, Margaret took a job teaching the first grade in a public school in Paterson, New Jersey, a factory town. It would have been a backbreaking job even for a veteran—and she was only a raw beginner. In her class there were eighty-four immigrant children—Poles, Hungarians, and Swedes—who could speak hardly a word of English. She was so tired at the end of the day she often collapsed on her bed and went to sleep before dinner. But she loved the challenge of opening the world of words and music and color to the children of the mill-workers. Then suddenly, at Christmastime, she was summoned home. Her mother was critically ill.

Anne Higgins had suffered from tuberculosis for so long that no one had expected this complete physical breakdown. Margaret found her terribly weak, coughing up blood constantly. To learn how to care for her mother, she borrowed medical books from the local doctor. She worked day and night in the sickroom; medicine was then unaware of how contagious tuberculosis was. There was nothing pleasant or easy about her tasks, yet she decided that here was a field where her strong yearning for service to others could be fulfilled. Instead of teaching, she would enter medicine.

Month after month she nursed her mother until she was exhausted herself. When one of her school friends invited her to Buffalo for Easter, Mrs. Higgins insisted that Margaret must take the rest. With Margaret gone, Anne Higgins thought of some pretext to send each child from the house. Michael, too, she prevailed upon to leave, to get some materials needed to repair the stove. A few blocks away, some deep instinct brought him running back in terror to find his wife gasping in death. Knowing she was about to die, she had wanted to spare the family this ending.

Margaret hurried home from Buffalo. Her words could not comfort her father. He had shut himself off, holding his grief tight. She took her mother's place now, running the household, managing the meals, the children, and even the debts. Burdened with problems, she found her hardest one was her father. Always gentle and loving before, urging his children to be free, he had turned into a petty tyrant through grief and anxiety. The younger boys had to be in bed the moment their lessons were done. The girls—Margaret and her sister Ethel—were kept practically prisoners. He tried to cut them off from everyone, particularly from boys.

Often when Margaret asked if a young man could call at the house, her father replied curtly, "No!" No explanation. That was the end of it. On the rare evenings when Margaret and Ethel were allowed out, they had to be home by ten and account for every minute away.

The climax came one night when the sisters had gone to an open-air concert. As the clock in the town hall struck ten, they were frantically running, still a few blocks from the house. When they reached the door, three minutes late, it was locked and the house was pitch-black. They knocked and banged and shouted, tried side and back doors. All were locked. Finally the front door opened a foot. Higgins reached out, took Ethel's arm, and pulled her into the house, snapping,

"This outrageous behavior is your sister's fault!" Then he slammed and locked the door, leaving Margaret, bewildered and stunned, alone on the dark porch.

She sat on the steps for a while, but it was a cool night and she had no coat. She started to walk, but no decent girl would stay on the streets at this late hour. She did not even have a relative in town to turn to.

Finally she thought of a girl who had been at the concert, too. Her mother welcomed Margaret in for the night. The next morning Margaret decided she had to give her father time to think over their relationship. She borrowed the fare from her hosts and took the train to Elmira, where she went to stay with friends. Meanwhile, Higgins had been desperately searching the town for her. When he learned where she was, he got her older sisters, Mary and Nan, now living in Buffalo, to wire her to return home at once. But Margaret refused to budge. She insisted on waiting out the week so that her father would try to understand the gulf that had opened between them.

After her return home, she and her father spoke little to each other. They buried themselves in their reading, he in his economics and politics, she finding relief in novels he always scorned as "trivial."

One afternoon, deep in a funny story and laughing aloud over it, she failed to hear her father enter the room. He stood in the doorway like a policeman, angry that someone was having a good time. She looked up at him, and suddenly all the love for him that had been pushed down inside her for so long by his icy harshness welled up again, and she laughed and laughed until her laughter drew him close. "Just listen to this," she said, reading him a passage from the book. Her father began to chuckle, and then to laugh, and then to roar with delight. He had found the way back to himself again.

Margaret realized why he had changed so much. He had been desperately lonely for Anne, for her quiet affection, her deep understanding. He had always depended on her to guide the children, and with her gone he had been scared by the size of his own responsibilities. And though he had probably never admitted it to himself, he had been jealous of the attention Margaret and Ethel had been given by their young men, wanting to keep his daughters all to himself. His cold discipline had simply been a reaction to this jealousy.

Margaret had grown far beyond such close controls. Neither Corning nor the family circle could hold her any longer. There was only one thing she wanted now—to become a doctor. A year after her mother's death, a Claverack classmate invited her to live in her family's house in White Plains, a suburban town just north of New York City. Nearby was the new White Plains Hospital, where Margaret could enroll as a probationary nurse. She did not yet have the money to go on to college and a medical degree. But this would start her on the way.

4. HUSBAND, HOUSE, AND BABIES

Training for her new work, Margaret made the mistakes most beginners make. On one of her first cases an old man called her to his bedside and asked her to bandage his sore leg. She had just learned bandaging and was delighted to put her new skill to work. Going the rounds a little later, her supervisor looked at the patient in astonishment and asked, "Why have you got the right leg bandaged? It's the left one that's injured."

"Oh, she was so kind," the old man replied, "I couldn't tell her she was working on the wrong one."

But Margaret learned fast. Her training was hard and unending. She had to carry supplies, make all the dressings and bandages, sterilize the equipment. The White Plains Hospital was in an old mansion. She slept in a tiny room under the roof. There was only one bathroom on each ward floor. No electricity, no bells to ring when you needed help quickly. At night the nurses were on their own, for no doctors were on duty then.

These hectic months of training, on top of the long period of nursing her own mother, were too much for her body to take. She developed tuberculosis and ran a temperature constantly. The doctors decided she needed an operation. Hardly out of bed, she was assigned to night duty. Every kind of emergency case seemed to occur on her night shift during the next three months. When it was over, she welcomed her transfer to a large hospital in New York for her postgraduate training.

She learned to work with the latest surgical techniques and equipment at Manhattan Eye and Ear. Then at Forty-first Street and Park Avenue, the hospital provided a reasonable amount of comfort for the nurses, including occasional social events. One night she was dancing with a young doctor when he was called out to the hall. He was building a house, and his architect had dropped by to show him some blueprints.

"This is William Sanger," the doctor said to Margaret. The architect was a dark slim man of medium height. They leaned over the blueprints. Whenever Margaret glanced up, she met Sanger's eyes fixed intensely on hers. She was on the late night shift, and had to go back to her ward. But at seven thirty in the morning, when she left the hospital, Sanger was standing there on the steps. He had waited all night to walk her home. And every morning after that, he was there. Impatient, romantic, he courted her feverishly. He sent flowers, bought her gifts, took her to the theater and the opera on her nights off duty.

To Margaret, raised on debts and budgets, it was like a make-believe world. What something cost never bothered Bill. While not wealthy, his family stood for the comfortable and educated world of the houses on the hill at Corning. Sanger was ten years older than Margaret, and had already moved into a large circle of musicians, artists, and writers.

Although he was helping to design important buildings, his real interest lay in painting. He was always talking of Paris, "the city of light," where a man could be free of business pressures and give himself up to learning to paint. "Let's get married and go there to live," he would urge her.

One day, without any warning, it happened. It was August 18, 1902—she was twenty-three years old. They were driving in the country when Bill suggested they stop to visit a friend of his. Without telling her, Bill had planned every detail—license, ring, witnesses, and the friend who turned out to be a minister. She found she didn't need to think about it, only to say yes.

The first year of marriage was happy. Then Margaret's tuberculosis flared up again. And now she was pregnant, too. She must go upstate to the Adirondack Mountains where the fresh air was considered healing. Bill insisted she stay at one of the hospitals near Saranac until it was time to have the baby. She returned to their Manhattan apartment in October 1903, just before the birth of their first son, Stuart.

Her labor pains started coming in the middle of the night. Neither her regular doctor nor his assistant could be reached. Bill rushed out to find any doctor he could. It was a young man he came back with. Because of his inexperience and Margaret's poor health, the delivery was long, hard, agonizing. But fortunately the baby was strong and healthy when born.

She felt so drained by the birth she had to return to the Adirondack clinic. Nothing seemed to stop the spread of her tuberculosis. In the next eight months she sank lower and lower, gradually losing even her interest in living.

Alarmed, her doctor came to examine her. "What would you like to do?" he asked.

"Nothing."

"Where would you like to go?"

"Nowhere."

"Who would you like to have take care of your baby?"

She did not even answer.

A little later the doctor returned, and putting his hand on her shoulder, shook her. "Don't be like this!" he said. "Do something! Want something! You'll never get well if you keep on this way!"

Something stirred in her. Not his words, but the sound of despair, of hopelessness, reached her.

She could not sleep that night. She knew now that everyone expected her to die soon. "I won't die, I won't," she kept whispering to herself.

By dawn she had decided what she must do. No matter what the doctor might say, she wanted to be at home with her husband. She got out of bed, called the nurse to get the baby ready, had her bags packed, and started home. It was a life-saving decision that came out of some mysterious reservoir of strength.

Bill moved his family into a small hotel in West-chester. With his constant love and care, Margaret slowly rebuilt her strength. They looked around for a place to start their own home and chose Hastings-on-Hudson. There, on a hillside over-looking the broad river, less than an hour from New York City, a group of doctors and artists calling themselves the Columbia Colony lived in small houses, with gardens, lawns, and plenty of space for their children to play. The Sangers rented a cottage while Bill designed a home for the acre of land they had bought.

It was to be the special home that every archi-tect dreams about. There would be a studio for him to paint in, a dining room big enough for many guests, fireplaces in all the bedrooms, with a huge one in the library, and finally a nursery—they had decided to have more children—open-ing out on a veranda overlooking the Hudson.

Margaret and Bill put in long hours together, staining the woodwork themselves, leading and welding together every bar of the rose window which was to set off the head of the staircase.

Now the new house was almost finished. The last of the plaster had yet to dry—and Margaret could not do too much, for she was carrying her second child—but they moved in anyhow. The boxes and crates were still half-full when they put tired Stuart to bed and relaxed in front of the roaring fire Bill had made to keep out the bitter cold of the February night.

It was hours later when Margaret heard a pounding on their bedroom door and the maid's voice yelling "Fire! Fire!" She ran to Stuart's bed while Bill raced down the stairs for help. Smoke was choking the rooms below, and flames were licking at the stairs, but Margaret, covering the baby's head with a coat, snaked her way past them to the open air. Outside, ice glittered on the moonlit trees. They stood helpless, watching the fire devour their home. A year of work was turning into ashes. Petal by petal, the treasured rose window vanished in the flames. In a few minutes its loveliness was gone.

It was time for sorrow, for rage at blind luck, for horror at how close death had come. Yet Margaret felt a sense of relief stealing over her. It was as if a burden had been lifted from her, as if a part of her life she had not known she wanted to end, was being ended for her. "Somewhere in the back of my mind," she wrote later, "I saw the absurdity of placing all one's hopes, all one's efforts, in the creation of something external that could perish in a few moments. I must have learned the lesson of the futility of material things."

The fire was a hard blow to them financially. Their insurance covered the house but not the furniture in it. They moved to a rented place nearby for the six months it took to rebuild the house.

Soon after the fire their second son, Grant, was born, and twenty months later, their daughter, Peggy. She was a lively, laughing girl, exactly what Margaret had wanted in a daughter. Margaret gave all her energy to rearing the children and even wanted a fourth, until her tuberculosis flared up again and the doctor warned against it.

Gradually, Margaret slipped into the round of suburban life. It was a closed-in world, women and children together all day long, the talk all of cooking, furniture, clothes, gardens, schools. The weekly trip to New York for shopping or a visit to a museum was the peak of excitement. Dissatisfied with the local kindergarten, the neighbors started their own, with Margaret taking her turn at teaching. When Stuart and his friends began to ask where babies came from, she put together a special course. With animals and nature to draw on, she taught them the simple facts about sex and biology.

But once the children were ready for school, suburban life began to seem trivial and empty. She was not satisfied endlessly to repeat the cycle of days. Restless, discontented, groping for something she could not define, she began reading widely. She felt out of the main current of life, and she was not alone in that. Everywhere in America, the quiet content of a generation ago was fading among well-to-do women. By 1910 their discontent was so common doctors and psychologists became openly concerned. The symptoms were familiar—boredom, tiredness, illnesses one couldn't explain, fits of crying without cause. "Nerves" or "melancholia," some called it. But others more acute said it was the response of middle- and upper-class women to useless idleness. They had servants to do the household work, and schools to educate their children. Their husbands did not need to have their wives work to piece out a decent income. Nothing much was left for such women but to consume—to buy and use the products of a flourishing industrial society. Many were satisfied with the role. But to others the life of the average leisure-class woman was boring and irritating.

Early on, encouraged by her father's example, Margaret had struggled with ideas. She had looked for adventure and challenge. Now, settled into middle-class routine, she felt she was living at second hand. Raising a family was not enough for her. It did not satisfy the urge to have a life of her own. The charming house, loving husband, beautiful babies—what the popular magazines said every woman hungered for—did not make her happy. She wanted to plunge into the world of action outside and use to the full powers she sensed were not yet tested in the small world of Hastings.

5. SLUMS AND STRIKES

From suburb to city Margaret went—a distance of approximately twenty miles. But it would make a vast change in her way of life. The Sangers moved into a roomy old apartment uptown on West 135th Street. Margaret wanted to make money on her own again to help with their expenses and debts, which had been heavy since her illness. So that she could go back to professional nursing, Bill's mother came to live with them. Margaret took only childbirth cases now. She would work hard for a couple of weeks while the children were in the safe hands of their grandmother. Then she would be at home again for a while before the next case.

Calls for her skilled nursing began pouring in. People did not use hospitals in those days except for severe emergencies. Most women preferred to have their babies at home. More and more, Margaret found herself going down to attend childbirths in the crowded tenements of the lower East Side. Nothing could have been farther from the green lawns and spacious homes of Hastings. Here below Fourteenth Street lived the immigrant poor—Italians, Jews, Irish, Germans—three thousand of them jammed into every square block of tenements. The hopefuls seeking a promised land had been flooding in ever since the late 1840s.

To help pay the rent, many families took in boarders. A single room would bed five or six sleepers. Thousands of apartments never saw a ray of sunlight. Windows were often narrow slits on airshafts filled with the stink of garbage. Many tenements had only one bathtub, sitting in the backyard. There was a toilet only on every other floor. Women dragged their garbage pails down five or six rickety flights to toss it on the steaming pile in the street.

In a typical block investigators counted 400 babies. Examining Health Department figures, Margaret saw the frightening toll the slums took —204 infants dying out of every 1,000 born. And more were always coming to life to meet the same quick end.

Pregnancy was almost a permanent condition in

these tenements. It was the wives of working people Margaret took care of—truck drivers, dishwashers, pushcart vendors, carpenters, small shopkeepers. They had put aside nickels and dimes for months to pay for a doctor and a nurse. They cared about their families, and they welcomed Margaret's help, often giving her their homemade jellies or gefüllte fish.

Each time she helped one of the frail, worn women to bear her child, the question would come a few days later, "What can I do to stop another baby? All the time I'm sick, and no money. I couldn't have another baby again!"

Margaret would explain the one or two simple methods that she knew. But the women said no, they were no use to them. These methods didn't work very well, to begin with. And they placed the responsibility upon the man, who sometimes didn't care what happened or forgot to use the method.

What these women really wanted was a method they could use themselves, a method that was sure to work. "Tell me the secret, please!" they cried. And when Margaret insisted she had no secret, this was all she knew, they would grow bitter and say, "It's the rich that know all the secrets."

Desperate to prevent still another pregnancy, the poor would often turn to abortion, which means detaching the growing egg by force from the wall of the mother's womb during the first few months after it has started to grow. Abortion could be very dangerous, particularly if the woman tried to do it herself. Margaret knew mothers who swallowed herb tea or more potent chemicals, doses passed on from generation to generation that had no real medical value. Others in trying to dislodge the egg, often hurt themselves so badly they ended up in a hospital. Some never came home.

In the slums, doctors—they called themselves that, but most were quacks without a medical license—set up offices as abortionists. Their attempts were often just as dangerous or useless as those of the women themselves. But the women would ask help of anybody and try anything. On Saturday nights Margaret would see scores of women, their shawls hiding their faces, lined up at these offices, putting their trust in the five-dollar quacks.

A few days later, Margaret would hear that Mrs. Zelinsky had been rushed to a hospital or Mrs. Bonanno had put her head into the gas oven. These were women she knew, women who shared her own hopes and fears, who wanted the same decent life she wanted for her own family.

It makes no sense, it makes no sense, Margaret would say. Thousands and thousands of these abortions in New York every year, and most of them could be avoided if the women had real methods to prevent pregnancy.

But what could be done? She lay awake at night, searching the dark for answers. Poverty and childbearing, childbearing and poverty. It was an endless circle the women were trapped in. Unless they could find a way out, they were worn out by thirty.

When Margaret finished a nursing job in the tenements, she felt that she was coming out of a nightmare. She got no satisfaction from working among the poor, such as some charitable ladies found. She hated the wretchedness and hopelessness.

Away from the lower East Side, she lived in a vastly different atmosphere. That first year in New York—it was 1912—there was an electric excitement in the air. In manners, morals, art, politics, a revolt was boiling up. Young men and women were deeply critical of the values their fathers had lived by. They turned their backs on convention and tradition. They wanted to break the old molds and shape a new and freer life. Progressives, socialists, anarchists, revolutionists of all kinds, were making up prescriptions for the future. The pages of the radical publications, such as the *Masses* and the Socialist newspaper, the *Call*, sizzled with attacks on big business, on corrupt politicians, on censorship, on conservatism. The talk was all of "new liberties" and the need to right social wrongs. Some believed in wiping out poverty and injustice by using the vote and passing better laws. Others wanted to sweep away the old and replace it with a brand-new social system. Still others put their faith in the integrity of the individual and thought it possible to educate all the people to the point where they could live the good life without need of laws or police.

Some of these ideas were familiar to Margaret. She had often listened to her father talking socialism. But then he had stood alone in Corning, and now she was plunged into the heart of this new ferment. Bill had long held socialist beliefs, but he had never been politically active. In New York their living room became a gathering place for his radical friends. They talked all night, while Margaret fed them and listened. She met John Reed, a brilliant young reporter just out of Harvard, who would make his reputation as the chronicler of the Russian Revolution. There was Big Bill Haywood, a one-eyed giant with a booming voice. He had swept across the country organizing hard-fought strikes for the Industrial Workers of the World, who advocated direct action to unify all workers, skilled and unskilled, in a single body rather than organize those in a single industry or craft by craft. There was Emma Goldman, the anarchist gadfly; Elizabeth Gurley Flynn, the young black-haired beauty who had turned from Catholicism to organizing for the IWW; and Mabel Dodge, the wealthy matron whose spacious drawing room at 23 Fifth Avenue became a center of the new movement.

Humanitarian by instinct and upbringing. Margaret was drawn to socialism as the means to end the misery of the slums. A democratic, cooperative society seemed to her the way to organize men's energies and talents, so that all would share equally in the good things this highly productive machine age could offer. She joined the Socialist party, working in Local Number 5. It met nights in rooms over a store, close by the Sanger apartment, to study economics and politics. Margaret was asked to go out and recruit new members among the neighborhood's workingwomen. She spent much time with their unions, especially the Irish in the laundry union and the Scandinavians in the housemaids' union.

That year a great strike of textile workers broke out in Lawrence, Massachusetts. The millworkers rose in passionate revolt. Making only six or seven dollars a week, they refused to take a wage cut. "Better to starve fighting than to starve working!" was their battle cry. Now, organized by the IWW, thousands of foreign-born workers, from twenty different countries, were picketing the mills. The city was an armed camp. In a battle between police and pickets a woman striker was killed. Big Bill Haywood rushed up from New York to help conduct the strike.

The bitter New England winds froze the pickets, and hunger haunted their families. The union had no treasury and the strikers no savings. Funds and food came from workers in other mill towns, but the children suffered badly. The strike committee decided to send the children to other cities where friends of labor would care for them.

Margaret, experienced in nursing and a friend of the IWW leaders, was asked to head the New York committee. She took a train up to Lawrence and found the children huddled in a large hall, shivering with the cold. Their clothes were shreds and patches. Their parents worked in one of the country's richest woolen mills, but only 4 of the 119 wore overcoats. Almost none had warm underwear.

Before they started out, she had the children given a medical examination. Raised on miserable diets, they were skinny and pathetic. Almost all had enlarged adenoids and inflamed tonsils. "Never in all my nursing in the slums had I seen children in so ragged and deplorable a condition," she wrote later. Through the icy wind the children ran to the railroad station. Arriving in Boston, they had no money for taxis and had to walk from the North to the South Station.

On the way to New York—the children singing workers' songs all the way—Margaret worried about what preparations had been made to house and feed them the first night. But when they came into Grand Central Station, thousands of men and women stood packed on the platform, pushing through the police lines to catch up the children in their arms and hoist them on their shoulders. Then, singing and laughing, they paraded down to Webster Hall on East Eleventh Street with band blaring, banners flying, and torches flaring in the dark.

At Webster Hall the children raced to the tables piled high with supper and stuffed it all down eagerly. Then each was bundled off by temporary foster parents to live in a home for the duration of the strike.

The children's dramatic exodus caught the nation's attention and sympathy. The Lawrence textile magnates were enraged; they feared the strike would go on and on. When another group of children assembled at the station to leave for Philadelphia, troops and police surrounded them, clubbed the children and their parents, and then arrested them.

The brutal attack led to a Congressional investigation of the strike. Many of the workers—some of them children—came to Washington to testify. Margaret, too, was asked to take the stand. She told the committee about the hungry children, the condition of their clothing, their bad health— all from careful notes she had kept on each child. The shy, attractive woman, speaking for mothers everywhere about the simple needs of children, captured the committee. Public opinion swung behind the strikers, and the millowners gave in to their demands. At the end of March the little "refugees" were back home, fattened up and dressed in warm new clothing.

Margaret had come to know and share the problems of many workingwomen. She learned they wanted something more than shorter hours and higher wages. Like the women on the lower East Side, they wanted to know how to prevent their families from mounting to six, eight, or ten children. What use was a dollar or two more in the pay envelope if there was always another mouth to feed?

"Poverty and large families seem to go hand in hand," Margaret pointed out at one meeting of

Local Number 5. "If the unions are fighting for better wages and hours, they should be equally concerned about the size of the workingman's family."

She began to feel that neither the feminists who fought for women's rights nor the unions nor even the radicals went to the real heart of the issue. Yes, the right to vote, the right to organize, the right to strike for better pay and hours—these were tremendously important. But did they touch the most vital part of a woman's life—childbearing?

6. WHAT EVERY GIRL SHOULD KNOW

Margaret worked so hard at Local Number 5 and at her nursing duties that she had little time at home. As she was about to leave the apartment one evening, her son Grant climbed on her lap and asked, "Are you going to a meeting?"

"Yes."

"A soshist meeting?"

"Yes."

"Oh, I hate soshism!" the little boy cried.

But the phone was always ringing to make more demands on her, and she found it hard to say no. One night it was the editor of the women's page of the Socialist newspaper, the *Call*.

"Will you help me out?" the editor asked. "We have a women's meeting tonight, and our speaker is sick."

"But I've never made a speech in my life," Margaret protested.

"You've got to this time. There's no one else we can call on."

Margaret finally agreed. She was so scared she couldn't eat her supper that night. What could she say? She was no expert on unions or socialism. But at Lawrence she had seen how wages and hours were closely tied to the size of a worker's family and its health. She would try to bring these problems into the open.

That night she climbed the dark stairs to the old meeting hall and walked fearfully into the room. There were only a handful of women there, slumped in their folding chairs after a day of hard work in the shops. With her wide-set gray eyes, her bright auburn hair pinned in coils around her head, Margaret seemed very young to them. She began slowly and softly. Then an inner current of excitement surged up, and her voice became more compelling. Now the women leaned forward, intent on every word. Talking about family health and its connection to work and wages, she struck straight at the heart of the problems that meant most to them. They wouldn't let her sit down afterward; she had to answer questions for hours.

So great was the demand for more discussion that the club arranged another talk. This time

Margaret spoke to seventy-five women. Other groups heard about it and begged her to come. As she talked with more and more women and saw how crushing their burden was, she felt guilty about her own comfortable family life. But what was the way out for them? How could she help?

One night, early in that summer of 1912, she was called to another grim tenement on the lower East Side, where a small, dark-haired woman named Sadie Sachs lay critically ill. Jake Sachs, a truck driver, had come home from work the night before to find his wife unconscious on the floor and his three small children helplessly crying. Mrs. Sachs, still in her twenties, had tried to abort herself, and septicemia—blood poisoning—had set in.

The doctor and Margaret struggled to save her. Day and night that hot July Margaret sweated in that tenement, carrying food and ice up three flights of stairs, hovering by the bedside with ice packs and drugs. After three weeks Mrs. Sachs was sitting up in bed.

At the doctor's last visit, Mrs. Sachs whispered, "Another baby will finish me, I guess."

"If you have another, there won't be any need to send for me," the doctor replied gently.

"But what can I do to stop it?" Mrs. Sachs pleaded.

The doctor had worked hard to save her life. But he had no practical answer. Quickly, with a kind of sour humor that came from handling hundreds of such cases, he said, "There's just one way. Tell Jake to sleep on the roof." And then he left.

Knowing that the doctor meant she could no longer have the normal relationship of love and tenderness with her husband, Mrs. Sachs turned to Margaret. "He can't understand," she whispered. "He's only a man. But you're a woman. You do. Please tell me the secret!"

What could Margaret say? A woman's life depended on the answer. All she could do was stand there, helpless, feeling silence was better than empty, comfortless words.

Margaret could not forget the pitiful figure of Mrs. Sachs. Her face haunted her as the weeks turned into months. Then the telephone rang one night, and it was Jake Sachs's voice begging her to come immediately. His wife was very sick again, and for the same reason.

Margaret hurried down, and found Mrs. Sachs in a coma, the doctor frantically trying to save her. But it was too late this time. In ten minutes she was dead. "I folded her still hands across her breast, remembering how they had pleaded with me, begging so humbly for the knowledge which was her right." Like a madman, Jake was tearing hair out of his head, moaning "My God! My God! My God!"

Margaret left the house, and walked the dead streets for hours, dreading to stop, fearing to face her own conscience. At three in the morning she was home again. She stood at the window, staring out over the city. Overflowing tenements . . . too

many children . . . babies dying in infancy . . .
children of six and seven forced to work in sweat-
shops . . . another baby on the way, and another,
and another. . . .

As the dark gave way to the morning sun Margaret knew she had come to a break with her
past. "There was only one thing to be done. The
doubts, the questioning, the experimentation,
were now put behind me. I knew I could not go
back merely to keeping people alive. I was
through with surface cures. Doctors must be
made to see the facts. Women must have knowledge of contraception, of the means to control the
size of their family. I would tell the world what
was going on in the lives of these poor women.
No matter what it should cost, I would be
heard."

On Sunday, November 17, 1912, readers of the
Call picked up their paper and were startled to
find the first of a remarkable series of articles
headlined "WHAT EVERY GIRL SHOULD
KNOW."

It was the first fruit of Margaret's determina-
tion to tell the world. Her purpose was to change
women's attitude toward sex and to emphasize
that "the procreative act is natural, clean, and
healthful." In language that anyone could understand, the twelve-part series described the changes
in female organs during the growth from childhood through adolescence, the functions of all
these organs in sexual life, and the dangers of
venereal disease.

Until now, no newspaper or magazine had dared to tell women the important facts about their own bodies. The reason for this silence was the wall of prudery and fear that had been piled stone on stone during the nineteenth century to shut sex away as a dirty secret. Almost everything about sex and the human body was unmentionable in those decades. In polite society, legs were always called limbs. The fake morality for some went to the ridiculous extreme of covering piano legs in ruffles.

The mind controlling this aspect of public discussion in the United States was Anthony Comstock's. The Connecticut-born man was founder and secretary for life of the New York Society for the Suppression of Vice. With a small group of fanatical followers, he had been able to get Congress in 1873 to pass an all-powerful censorship law known as the Comstock Act. (Some thirty states soon passed their own "little Comstock laws.") The Post Office Department made Comstock a special agent, giving him the power to open any letters, packages, pamphlets, or books going through the mails. He personally could therefore decide what was "lewd," "obscene," "indecent," "immoral." Since no one had drawn up any rules or guidelines as to what these words meant, Comstock alone was judge and jury of what could be sent through the mails.

Margaret's articles were being praised by health authorities, and thousands of women were asking for reprints. But Comstock decided that the article on gonorrhea, a disease acquired by

sexual contact, had upset public taste. The *Call*
was notified that if it printed Margaret's next
article—on syphilis, another venereal disease—its
mailing permit would be taken away.

Since a newspaper must have that permit to
survive, the *Call* did not run the article. But it
called attention to the fact that its readers were
being told what they could or could not read.
When they opened the issue of February 9, 1913,
they found the left side of the woman's page a
blank, except for the words:

WHAT EVERY GIRL SHOULD KNOW
NOTHING
by order of
THE POST OFFICE DEPARTMENT

The series resumed, and when finished, was
printed in pamphlet form so that it could reach
thousands more.

The real problem she faced, Margaret was
learning, was where to find the facts she needed
and how to get them through to the country. It
was now forty years since the passage of Comstock's law. He was still campaigning relentlessly
against "immorality" and had caused the conviction of countless persons. Druggists, hospitals,
even doctors, were afraid to give any advice on
preventing births—even if the life of the mother
would be seriously endangered by having another
child or the child might be born damaged or de-
formed.

Comstock even set traps for kind-hearted doctors. He had two women associates write to a Midwestern physician, claiming that their husbands were insane and that they feared any children might inherit the insanity. When the doctor wrote them some simple advice, Comstock had him arrested and sent to prison for seven years.

No wonder everyone was frightened. When Margaret went for advice to doctors she knew, they asked her to leave the office, refusing to discuss the subject. When she sought the help of feminists, they said wait till we get the vote. The radicals said wait till the revolution, then the new society will take care of that, too. Others said wait till women were more educated.

Wait, wait, wait. But she couldn't wait. How could she, when millions of Sadie Sachses desperately needed this information?

She set her course: she would challenge the Comstock law in the courts. She would break the law openly by publishing information in a newspaper or pamphlet of her own.

Now she turned to the libraries for the facts she wanted. She spent months ransacking the shelves of New York and Washington libraries, searching through long-buried volumes and complex medical texts. She burrowed through a mountain of writing.

The idea of limiting family size was not new, of course. Various methods of preventing birth had been used for thousands of years. One technique was mentioned in the Old Testament, another in an Egyptian manuscript written 3800 years ago. The medical literature of the ancient world, Margaret found, was filled with contraceptive methods. People in every culture had tried to control the size of families. Many could come up with nothing better than abortion or infanticide —the killing of the newborn. But they tried all kinds of substances or procedures: pine bark, tanned sumach, seaweed, root of spotted cowbane, castor beans, pomegranate peel, rue seed, thyme, parsley, myrtle, elephant dung, crocodile dung, cedar oil, cabbage blossoms, foam from a camel's mouth, stepping three times over a grave, holding the breath.

As she traced contraception into nineteenth-century America, Margaret discovered that the birth rate before the Civil War had been very high. But it was not because women wanted big families. Doctors recorded innumerable cases of women begging them for methods to stop having children. The trouble was the methods were no good.

Poor families relied mostly on "churchyard luck"—the high rate of infant mortality. In those prewar decades, four out of five children died before reaching the age of five years.

Margaret came across the first treatise on birth control to be published in America. It was Robert Dale Owen's *Moral Physiology*. As a frontispiece Owen printed a picture of a young woman abandoning her baby at a foundling hospital; the caption said, "Alas! that it should ever have been born." Owen assured his readers that limiting the number of their children would make both husband and wife happier and their marriage richer. His methods, however, were inadequate unless husband and wife showed great care and restraint.

A year later, in 1832, the first practical pamphlet appeared. Written by a courageous Massachusetts doctor, Charles Knowlton, it was called *The Fruits of Philosophy: or, The Private Companion of Young Married People*. Its publisher was sent to jail for it, but the uproar over the censorship made the pamphlet a best seller for the next ten years.

Knowlton warned that a mother's health was drained by having too many children. But his most important section was a description of four methods of contraception.

The process of birth starts with the sexual act, when the penis of the father carries his sperm into the mother through her vagina. The, sperm unites with the egg within the mother in a special place called the uterus. A cluster of cells grows in the uterus, developing into the baby within nine months. The vagina is the same passageway through which the baby is born after the nine-month growing period in the mother's uterus.

Contraception, therefore, depends on preventing the sperm from reaching the egg. Today we have several complex and dependable means of doing this. But in 1913, when Margaret began her search for information, the few simple methods

known were the same as those outlined by Knowlton eighty years earlier.

The first method, he said, was "withdrawal."
During the sexual act, the man had to withdraw
his penis from the woman before he deposited
his sperm in her body, thus preventing the sperm
from reaching the egg. The main problems were
that during the act of love-making, the man could
forget to do this. And above all, it put the responsibility on the man; Margaret believed it
should belong to the woman.

Second, said Knowlton, was the male sheath or
condom (used since the eighteenth century). It
was a thin rubber covering, slipped over the
penis before the sexual act, which prevented the
sperm from entering the woman's body and reaching the egg. Again a problem was dependability
(since the sheath could break or slip off during
use), and here, too, the responsibility was the
man's.

The third and fourth methods Knowlton described involved the woman's use of a sponge to
block the sperm or of chemical solutions to wash
the sperm out.

The main trouble, Margaret thought, was that
Knowlton did not describe the last two methods
—where the woman was in control—in detail.
Further, Margaret could not depend on information so old, and she had no proof of how effective
or safe it was.

The months of research had tired her out. And
Bill and the children were complaining of her long

absences from home. That summer of 1913, they decided, would be spent on a long family vacation, away from all distractions. They took a cottage on the windswept dunes near Provincetown, on Cape Cod. Bill worked at his painting, and Margaret gave all her attention to the children. They had sunrise breakfasts and sunset picnics on the dunes, swam in the cold sea, and roved the great beaches day after day.

But as she played and rested, Margaret could not forget her work. One day, talking to Bill Haywood, the labor leader, who had come to visit, she described the problems of her research. "Don't stay here," he said. "Get your information at the source. The women of France have been limiting their families for generations. Go to France to get your answers."

A wonderful idea, she thought—and it would give Bill Sanger what he had long desired—the chance to paint in Paris instead of building dull suburban homes. They agreed to make any sacrifice to finance the trip. They sold the Hastings house, took their combined savings out of the bank, and booked passage for Europe.

7. PARIS: END OF A MARRIAGE

When they reached Paris they took an apartment on the Boulevard St. Michael. Across the way was the Luxembourg Gardens where Stuart, Grant, and Peggy could play. Bill found a studio on Montparnasse, and while the children were at school, Margaret began to search the city for the facts she needed.

Even in the poorest working-class districts, she found knowledge of contraception widespread. "Have you just learned about it?" she would ask the women she met.

"Oh, no. *Maman* told me."

"Who told her?"

"*Grandmère,* of course."

Margaret soon learned that since 1807, when Napoleon decreed that family property must be divided equally among all the children, the thrifty workers and peasants had decided to limit their families, so that property would not shrink into too many bits and pieces. The small family had become an accepted standard in French life. Many unions and the radical political parties supported family limitation openly and distributed information on it to their members.

Methods of contraception, she learned, were passed on from generation to generation. This knowledge was considered as important to a girl as her ability to cook and run a house. From the doctors, midwives, and druggists she talked to, Margaret collected the best methods of using sponges and the solutions they should be soaked in, and the way to prepare and use douches, which carry water into the vagina to clean it. Both were methods Dr. Knowlton had described in general terms in his pamphlet.

But what she particularly wanted from the doctors and druggists were new devices to prevent conception—the diaphragm and the pessary. These had been developed about thirty years before by Dutch and German doctors who were not satisfied with the old methods. Both were small devices, generally made of rubber stretched over an adjustable ring, which the woman could place at the mouth of her uterus. Used along with medical jellies and other prescriptions, they were

safe and quite effective in preventing the sperm
from reaching the egg.

Margaret bought a good supply of these devices and stored them in her trunk along with
careful notes on everything she had gathered from
her interviews. At last she had the information
she needed. There was no point in lingering in
Paris; she was wasting time. She had to get back
home with her message. "I had practically
reached the exploding point. I could not contain
my ideas. I wanted to get on with what I had to
do in the world."

Could she ask Bill to return to America now?
He was very happy at his painting and deserved
the chance to stay in Paris. It had been very hard
on him, with all the time she had spent away
from home. She realized more and more how divided her life had become, split between family
and this work that was consuming her. She suggested she return to New York, taking the children, and Bill agreed.

They both knew they had slowly moved into
separate worlds. Their twelve years together had
been good. But now Bill felt more and more cut
off. The last year had seen Margaret spending
so much of her time at meetings, doing research,
writing, making speeches. True, Bill had encouraged her in the beginning, been proud of the
recognition she earned. But it left little time for
the role of wife. The house, domestic details—
she lost patience with them. Her goals, she felt,
had enlarged far beyond Bill's understanding.

It had simply turned out this way, and there was little she could do—or wanted to do—to change it. Slowly she was becoming the voice of a new freedom for women. She might even have to sacrifice husband and home, and to some extent, her children—so that she could fulfill this role as a crusader for a cause still struggling to be born. It was a terrible choice, for she hated every minute away from the children. But this cause, this work, possessed her. And like many champions of an idea before her, she had to do it no matter what the personal pain and loss.

In a sense, she was giving up her own marriage to help millions of other women and children. Some may have thought it a selfish choice, but in the larger picture of human progress, she was working for the benefit and happiness of countless others.

On the last day of 1913, Margaret said good-bye to Bill, and sailed for New York with the children. While she and Bill may not have realized it at the time, they would never again live together as husband and wife.

8. WOMAN REBEL

"To look the world in the face with a go-to-hell look in the eyes." That was Margaret's idea of a woman's duty—printed bold on the pages of her new monthly newspaper, the *Woman Rebel*.

As soon as she returned from Paris, she had settled with the children in a small apartment at the northern tip of Manhattan. Then, fired with the vision of a newspaper that would let voiceless women express themselves, she got to work. She had almost no money, but she refused to worry about it. "I do things first," she said, "and somehow or other they get paid for." Salaries would amount to little, for she took unto herself the jobs of editor, circulation manager, treasurer, and bookkeeper. The editorial offices were her dining room; the desk, her table. She looked to contributions—a dollar here and a dollar there—to keep the paper alive.

In March 1914 the first issue of the *Woman Rebel* appeared. True to its name, the paper sounded the call for revolt against the past. Its eight pages rang with such phrases as "a woman's body belongs to herself alone" and "enforced motherhood is the most complete denial of a woman's right to life and liberty."

She launched her new movement to support the use of contraception. But what should it be called? Sitting with a few friends one night, she debated a list of possibilities: family limitation, voluntary parenthood, the new motherhood. None sounded right. They were too big or too pompous or too vague.

They were considering "birth-rate control" when someone suggested they drop the "rate." Birth control it was, then, a name that had just the right sound and meaning. It would capture the imagination, and soon become a household phrase featured on the front pages of newspapers around the world.

Margaret sent copies of the *Woman Rebel* to the unions, to the Socialists, to every feminist group. She built a mailing list of two thousand, and thousands more copies were handed out at factory gates, at women's rights and radical meetings.

The paper struck fire at once. One speaker alone sold five hundred copies at a Los Angeles meeting. During the first months of publication Margaret got over ten thousand letters, most pleading for specific birth control information. But many people, too, were horrified by its frankness. A Pittsburgh paper, for instance, described the *Woman Rebel* in one sentence: "The thing is nauseating."

On April 2, while the first issue was being distributed, Anthony Comstock struck back. The Post Office Department wrote Margaret to say the March issue was "unmailable." She had expected it, and yet she was startled. For the first issue did not print a single line on contraceptive methods. It only supported birth control on principle and gave no advice to the readers. That did not seem to break the Comstock law.

Time was the important thing now. She must get out all the issues she could before she was summoned to face trial. She knew the risk—a possible prison term of five years and a fine of five thousand dollars.

She went ahead. Only half the first issue had been taken by the Post Office and destroyed. She and her friends sat up all night, typing new address labels, and by dawn were posting the paper, a few copies at a time, in mailboxes all over town.

Then three more issues—May, June, July— were banned by the Post Office. Each time she demanded to know just which articles broke the law. The government never answered.

Now, faced with certain court action, she decided to go further. She would answer the readers of her newspaper who were pleading for specific information. She would tell them about the methods of birth control. She went to work on a pamphlet she called *Family Limitation*. Its style was simple, direct, calm. She described what she had learned in Europe about douches, sponges, solutions, and the new diaphragms, with drawings that would help any woman to apply the knowledge. It was the first popular modern handbook on birth control—and it was a direct challenge to the Comstock law.

Margaret took the manuscript to a printer. He was a liberal, and a brave man. He read it and handed it back. "You'll never get this printed in New York," he said. "It means Sing Sing."

She went to printer after printer, twenty in one week. "I'd like to set it," they'd say, "but I have a family. I'd be in jail the minute it came out."

At last she found a man, a linotype operator on a foreign-language newspaper. He agreed to sneak back into the shop at night, and set it secretly. She arranged to have the printing and binding done by other men, none known to the others.

She had planned to print ten thousand copies, but as word got out and unions and other organizations sent in big orders, she raised the first printing to a hundred thousand. Night after night she and a few associates worked to wrap, weigh, and stamp bundles of the pamphlet. She sent them to friends in the labor movement all over the country, with orders to hold them until she found the right moment for distribution.

Meanwhile, news of what Margaret was doing had reached Corning. Michael Higgins held a family council. Had Margaret gone crazy? They feared she had suffered a mental breakdown. Higgins came down to New York to bring his daughter home.

Margaret told her father quietly about her work, her plans, her hopes. For days they talked, but she could not overcome his disgust. How could a decent young woman talk and write about sex? Was she crazed on the subject? Had her nursing experience coarsened her mind? Stamping angrily up and down her room, he shouted that he hated the *Woman Rebel;* he despised the people he saw coming to her house; he had no use for birth control, whatever it was. With the same thundering voice that had once praised Robert Ingersoll and Henry George, he was now damning his daughter's radicalism.

The argument went on and on. Then one August afternoon, Margaret's doorbell rang, and she opened the door to find two strange men waiting for her. They thrust an official document into her hand. Out of the mass of legal language leaped the central fact: she had been indicted on nine charges of violating the Comstock law. If found guilty on all counts, she could go to prison for forty-five years.

The two Justice Department agents did not

look like bad men. She wanted them to understand, though it would change nothing. She asked them in, and for hours talked of birth control, of what it could mean to women like Sadie Sachs, ground down by poverty and endless childbearing. They agreed that in the face of these tragedies the law was cruel. But it *was* the law, and it stood until it was changed. Nothing could be done about her indictment.

When the agents left, Higgins came in and put his arms around Margaret. Listening in the next room, he had heard everything. And now he understood. "You were right," he said. "Everything is on your side—common sense, progress, everything. If your mother had only known about birth control, she'd be alive today."

Margaret was moved by her father's words. If he could be convinced, a judge could, too. All she needed was the chance to explain what her movement was for, and everything would be all right.

A hearing in court took place on August 25. The district attorney wanted the trial held immediately. But the judge agreed to postpone it for six weeks.

There was little time to plan for an uncertain future. The children were at camp or visiting friends. She made arrangements for their schooling to continue. Then she rushed to finish the September and October issues of the *Woman Rebel*. She felt more and more alone. The first guns of a great war had shattered Europe's peace that August. Americans feared they would be drawn into it. The whole world's attention was focused on the battlefronts. Her act of defiance seemed very unimportant now. The People versus Margaret Sanger. Millions against one. How could she defend herself?

Help came. Lawyers from the unions and the Free Speech League called to offer their services. They could get her off on some technicality, they said, if she would cooperate with the court.

Cooperate?

They didn't understand. She wasn't concerned for her own safety. A prison term was not the issue. It was the Comstock law—*that* was the issue. The law was wrong, harmful, evil. If she "cooperated," she would be saying birth control was only some other form of obscenity or pornography. She did not want to go to jail, but she would if it would demonstrate how degrading this law was that kept women in bondage. Sensing the drama in the situation, she was ready to become the symbol of rebellion against the Comstock law.

On October 20, she was back in court. She asked for a postponement of another month. The judge said no, get a lawyer and appear for trial tomorrow morning.

She rushed to one lawyer who represented unions. He agreed to take her case. "I'm sure I can make a deal with the district attorney, so you'll plead guilty and only have to pay a fine," he assured her.

He didn't understand. Like the others, he

wanted only to get her off. He didn't care about the issue.

She called Bill Sanger. He was just back from Paris. Although living apart, they remained good friends. "Follow that lawyer's advice," he begged. "Let him get you off."

She had to be alone to think it through. She went home, packed a bag, and took a room in a small hotel. She knew that if she appeared in court the next day she would be convicted of publishing an "obscene" newspaper. People could think of little but the war in Europe. The Germans were advancing on Paris. Who was going to worry about birth control or civil rights?

What she needed was time: time to assemble her facts, time to rally women behind her, time to prove that birth control must be separated from "obscenity."

She thought of fleeing to England or Holland where the birth control movement was making rapid progress. But how could she leave her children? What would her associates think? Would they call it desertion? Would they understand? The minutes flew by as she wrestled with her decision. "It was a terrible moment," she said, long afterward. "Even now it sickens me to think about the struggle within me. But I had to go. I had to fight this through even if it meant leaving children, home, friends, everything I held dear."

Swiftly she wrote letters to the district attorney and the judge, explaining her decision not to stand trial. She arranged with Bill for the children to live with him, with her sister Nan to look after them.

Then she boarded a train for Montreal. Riding north, she wrote another letter to be mimeographed and sent to all the subscribers of the *Woman Rebel:*

"Shall we who have heard the cries and seen the agony of dying women respect the law which has caused their deaths? Jail has not been my goal. There is special work to be done and I shall do it first. If jail comes after, I shall call upon all to assist me. In the meantime I shall attempt to nullify the law by direct action and attend to the consequences afterward."

At Montreal she found a Canadian liner about to sail for England. She boarded the ship, wondering how long it might be until she would see home again.

9. LEARNING FROM EUROPE

Three days out at sea, Margaret cabled four trusted friends. A key word instructed them to release the hundred thousand copies of *Family Limitation* which had been hidden in storerooms and closets in a dozen cities. She would not learn for months what the effect would be, but with this message she made her exile final.

Up to this point, she could have argued that the *Woman Rebel* had only challenged the Comstock law. But *Family Limitation* openly broke the law. No one had dared do this before. Others had argued for contraception on principle. She now defied the law to give the public detailed information on all the methods.

In London she rented a small room near the British Museum, whose magnificent library she planned to use. The room had no heat, and every night she went to bed chilled to the bone. Mornings at seven a knock at the door would wake her. She would rise to find ice formed in the pitcher and a little jug of hot water outside. She would mix the two and wash. There was but one bathroom in the house, and the landlord charged for its use.

The first people she wanted to meet in London were Dr. C. V. Drysdale and his wife, Bessie. For sixty years one Drysdale after another had led the British movement for population control. She sent a note to them and was at once invited to tea. In their bright living room, warmed by a blazing fire and their friendship, she felt her loneliness lift. They stuffed her with good food and good talk, asked a hundred questions about her struggle in America. When Dr. Drysdale heard the details, he exclaimed, "If we only had a Comstock law to rouse British opinion! There's nothing like a bad law to stir the British!"

They gave her the run of their private library, and showed her the valuable reports their movement had collected. Now she began going every day to the British Museum, taking her reserved seat in the reading room at nine, and seldom leaving until the closing at seven.

Following the suggestions of the Drysdales, she read the important books on the British movement. It was Thomas Malthus in 1803, she learned, who first spoke out for population control. He had studied the figures on population increase and found that in many places, such as rural America, the birth rate was doubling every fifteen years. Then he noted that as deaths from war and famine decreased, and people lived longer as a result of better conditions, the brakes that had kept population low for thousands of years were being removed. The result, he predicted, would be vast increases in population that would soon outpace the amount of food available and even the land for living space.

Francis Place, a Londoner who started out by making leather breeches and ended as a great labor leader, was the first to bring birth control into the open for public discussion. In 1822 he published a little pamphlet called *To The Married of Both Sexes of The Working People*. In clear words he told women how they could avoid having more children than they wanted. Place, himself the father of fifteen children, thought the birth of too many children in workers' families was a threat to their bargaining power. With a surplus of labor, wages would go down, he feared.

About ten years later, Dr. Knowlton's pamphlet and the Owen book gave Americans the first simple descriptions of contraceptive techniques.

But why did these books have so little effect in America? Searching for clues in history, Margaret found some answers. There was the rigid

Puritan sense of morality, first of all. It made any
talk of sex impossible. No wonder Knowlton's
publisher went to jail. But more important, perhaps, was the fact that no matter how many people were being born or were coming in as immi-
grants, there was plenty of room for all. America
was a vast country. The open lands of the West
could hold millions of farmers. And the giant fac-
tories that sprang up after the Civil War were
hungry for more and more workers.

It was not until the turn of the century that
things began to change. Higher standards of living, better education for more people, the mech-
anization of industry, began to make people
think differently. A desire for smaller families was
a natural outcome.

Margaret turned up one surprising fact. Although Dr. Knowlton's 1832 booklet had been for-
gotten in America, it was printed in London in
1876. The publishers were arrested and convicted
of harming public morals. They appealed the
case, supported by a wave of newspaper headlines, and won. Their victory meant that in England there was no longer anything illegal in publishing information about contraception. In the
next few years the book sold over three hundred
thousand copies, and England's birth rate dropped
rapidly.

In her research Margaret had often used a
giant seven-volume work called *Studies in the
Psychology of Sex.* Over tea at the Drysdales' one
afternoon, they told her they would introduce her

to the author of the book, Havelock Ellis. He would have an immeasurable influence on her thinking and action, not just at this time, but for the rest of her life.

Ellis was now fifty-five, a tall gaunt man with a massive head, sad blue eyes, and a shock of white hair. His *Psychology of Sex,* a pioneering work, was the most important book in the field so far. He believed that "sex lies at the root of life, and we can never learn to reverence life until we know how to understand sex."

Ellis and Margaret became friends, meeting often and going to concerts together. He guided her studies at the British Museum for the rest of her stay. When they were apart, he sent her a stream of notes. One cautioned her: "No one rebel or many rebels can crush law by force. It needs skill even more than strength." And another read: "I know you are not happy unless you are doing something daring."

Between the two a rare intimacy grew that went beyond their work. She saw in him a spirit that embraced everything that was human. He was no organizer of change who went into the streets with his message. But his wisdom was so deep, his voice so serene, that he kindled minds everywhere.

Her work in the library made Margaret realize that she must go to the Netherlands to study at first hand the world's first chain of birth control clinics. Reports showed that the birth rate there had been cut about a third. The country had the

lowest rate of mothers' deaths while the United
States had one of the highest. And the infant
death rate in the three cities where the clinics
operated was the lowest in the world.

Tied to the low birth rate were steadily improving working conditions and wages. The benefits
had proved so great that Queen Wilhelmina had
given the clinics a royal charter and a medal of
honor. Here was a government—the exact opposite of the American—which considered birth
control information not an "obscenity" but a constructive force.

Making the Channel crossing in January 1915
despite the danger of submarines and mines,
Margaret went to The Hague. She was welcomed
by the founder of the clinics, Dr. Johannes Rutgers. For two weeks she watched the doctors and
nurses give instruction in contraception. After her
painful battles at home it was astounding, she
said, to find that here "contraception was looked
upon as no more unusual than we in America
look upon the purchase of a toothbrush."

The most important thing she learned was that
the clinic trained each patient in the method that
suited her best. If Dr. Rutgers prescribed a diaphragm, for instance, the patient was fitted for
one of fourteen different sizes and then carefully
taught its use.

Margaret learned swiftly, and was allowed to
advise and fit patients herself. Before her visit was
over, she attended seventy-five women. Her experience gave her knowledge of the principles by

which to guide the American clinics that would one day be established. The clinics must have a skilled medical staff, with contraception taught only by doctors and nurses.

She understood now that the birth rate was not the only important factor in the health of the family and community. Mothers had also to learn to space their children, to make sure they were born two or three years apart. With proper spacing a mother could recover her health and strength between births.

That spring she was back in London. Friends arranged for her to tell British audiences what she had learned in Holland. To civic and social groups she introduced the words "birth control," and the need to establish medical clinics for its practice.

By midsummer her small savings were running out. Worse, a strange fear began to haunt her— the fear that something was wrong with her daughter, Peggy. True, Bill Sanger and her sister Nan wrote every week. And their reports on the children's health and schooling were reasuring. But still Margaret was troubled by some deep sense of danger. It was a kind of mystical feeling that would often seize her. She would wake in the night, hearing Peggy's voice crying, "Mother, Mother, are you coming back?" Then a letter would arrive from New York to tell her all was well. Still the dreams would come again. And somehow the date—November 6—stamped huge on a calendar, would swim up in her mind.

In the last months she had been greatly encouraged by letters from friends on the birth control movement at home. "The whole atmosphere is changing for the better," the Free Speech League wrote her. If she were tried now, the case would not be ignored. "Everybody in the country will know what is happening."

In August she heard from a union leader who had just returned from a swing around the country. Interest in birth control was tremendous, he wrote. In the Chicago stockyards district alone, women had snatched up five hundred copies of her pamphlet. He urged her to come home and start on a nationwide speaking tour.

There was another reason for her to go back. Bill Sanger had been arrested. A "Mr. Heller" had visited Bill's studio, pleading that he was a poor man with too many children. Wouldn't Bill give him a copy of *Family Limitation?* Fishing one out of a drawer, Bill handed it over. A few days later "Heller" came back with a tall man in muttonchop whiskers, who said, "I am Mr. Comstock. I have a warrant for your arrest."

Bill was held in jail for thirty-six hours before bail could be secured. He was told that if he would reveal where Margaret was, he would get off. He wrote Margaret that he had answered, "You can wait till hell freezes over before that will happen!"

When the trial opened in September, Bill told the crowded courtroom that he knew he had broken the law, but it was the law, and not he, that was on trial. Justice McInerney broke in to say, "The pamphlet is not only contrary to the laws of the State but contrary to the laws of God. Any man or woman who would circulate literature of this kind is a menace to the community."

The judge gave Bill a choice: a $150 fine or thirty days in jail.

"I would rather be in jail with my self-respect and manhood than be free without it!" Bill cried.

A storm of clapping and shouting and cheering swept the courtroom as Bill was led off to jail.

The news of Bill's trial ended Margaret's indecision. With Bill in prison—and he had never been involved in her movement—how could she stay away any longer? She had to go back to take up the fight against the savage law that had trapped Bill and still threatened her. To make more and more people understand, she would carry her message to the country.

There were her children, too, separated now from both father and mother. She was desperately lonely for them. She booked passage at once and sailed in late September.

The crossing was made in fog and fear. Every passenger was thinking of the *Lusitania,* the great ship the Germans had torpedoed. Margaret was sunk in gloom. "The ship was carrying me onward, onward, to disaster, to prison, to inevitable sorrow." The frightening date, November 6, still tormented her. She could not shake off a queer sense of evil.

On a gray October morning the ship pulled into New York harbor. No one stood on the dock to welcome her. But suddenly the cold fog that had settled on her heart lifted its grip. She was breathing the air of home again; she was looking at American faces, faces that did not know the despair of war-torn Europe; she was hearing the familiar voices of longshoremen and cabdrivers and porters. It made her unbelievably glad. She wanted the feeling to last, so she picked up her one small bag and walked away from the pier.

Passing a newsstand, she noticed the cover of *Pictorial Review*, a leading magazine of the time. Streaming across it was the title of the featured article, "What Shall We Do About Birth Control?" How wonderful it was to be welcomed home by words of her own making, the very words that had sent her into exile twelve long months ago.

10. OBSCENITY—OR FREE SPEECH?

Home again, there was a whole year to make up for. Everyone talked at once, wanting to know what each minute lived apart had been like. Margaret saw that Stuart, just entering his teens, was bigger and huskier than she remembered him. He charged around the apartment with his football, hurling forward passes at armchairs. Grant, serious and shy, still tagged after Peggy, whose laughter always filled the house.

But the time to play was pitifully short. Immediately ahead was the trial Margaret had returned to face. She needed to find people to back up her fight and money to finance it. She turned

first to the National Birth Control League, under
new leadership since her exile. Their answer
stunned her. The league, they said, aimed to
change the laws, not to break them. How can
they talk of "wrong tactics," Margaret thought,
while women die senselessly because of the Comstock law?

She turned to the doctors. The New York Academy of Medicine had a committee looking into
birth control. Surely they would help? No, they
said, they needed more time. She thought they
needed more courage. Then who, what, was left?
She had almost no money—either for her trial or
for the family's living expenses.

And then, with terrible suddenness, the worst
blow fell. Peggy came down with pneumonia.
There were no sulfa drugs, no penicillin, in those
days, to fight the infection. For two weeks, first
at her apartment, then at the hospital, Margaret
never left Peggy's side. Her sister Ethel, a nurse,
too, gave her constant help. Peggy's resistance
failed rapidly. Passing her days and nights in deep
sleep, she would open her eyes for a moment
and whisper, "Are you back, Mother? Are you
back from London?"

"I'm right here, darling."

But the child kept repeating, "Are you really
back?"

They were almost the same words that had
haunted Margaret in London when that date,
November 6, had imprinted itself on her mind.
The hours dragged by, terrible hours, the worst

in her life. Then a moment more—and Peggy was gone.

Nothing would ever affect Margaret so deeply as her daughter's death. Hours later she realized that the date was November 6. She could not think. Her mind was locked in her loss. A great gulf of loneliness set her apart from the rest of the world. For years after Peggy's death it was impossible for Margaret to sit opposite a child in a bus or train. Tears would fill her eyes, and she would have to move to another seat.

News of Peggy's death, coming on the eve of the trial, reached the country through the newspapers. Consoling letters poured in on Margaret, many containing small contributions to her defense fund. The district attorney offered to postpone the trial, but she insisted it be held in December.

Worried for her health and fearing she could not stand up under a trial, friends pleaded for her to compromise. Lawyers sounded out the district attorney and advised Margaret she could get off with a suspended sentence if she would plead guilty. You've made enough sacrifices, they said. But she refused to do it. Then Samuel Untermyer, the noted liberal lawyer, stepped in. He talked to the district attorney, too. "You don't even have to go into court," he reported to Margaret. "Just write a letter saying you won't break the law again, and the case will be dropped."

Again, compromise. It was always the same.

"I'm not concerned about going to jail," Margaret insisted. "The question is whether I have or have not done something obscene. If I have not, I cannot plead guilty."

Then it was that she decided to dramatize the issue. She would appear in court without a lawyer. She would stand alone against the federal government, defying a stupid law as a woman speaking with the voice of all women. Not defense, but attack! That would be her weapon. She was sure the whole country would understand it.

Her decision rallied support at once. A group of prominent women petitioned the judge to have half the jury made up of women. Nine of England's most brilliant men—headed by H. G. Wells and Arnold Bennett—signed a letter to President Wilson in behalf of birth control and free speech. Hundreds of distinguished Americans, who only weeks before had called Margaret too radical, attended a defense dinner for her.

On January 18, 1916, when the trial opened in the federal court, the crowd of Margaret's supporters was so huge that hundreds overflowed into the corridors. Reporters and photographers jammed the press tables. Then the district attorney astonished everyone by asking the judge to postpone the case for a week. Margaret rose in protest, but the judge overruled her. A week later—another postponement. It was plain that the government was having second thoughts. Public opinion was swinging behind Margaret. The war news dominated the headlines, but Margaret's case still made its way onto the front pages. *Pictorial Review* reported that 97 percent of the thousands of letters received in response to its article on birth control were favorable. Realizing how strong sentiment in her favor was becoming, the district attorney asked for another postponement, and another, and finally, on February 18, the government dismissed the case.

What had been proved? Nothing—in legal terms. Nonetheless, Margaret had won an important victory. Fighting alone, she had forced the press to discuss the issue of birth control. And the public now knew that talk of contraception was not a matter of obscenity. It belonged in the public forum.

Her friends crowded around, congratulating her on a great victory. Underneath their warm words, however, she sensed the unspoken feeling that she ought to settle down now, take her husband back, and give herself up completely to family life.

Margaret could not accept that. She had won a moral victory, but the law was still to be tested. And besides, this was more than a free speech movement. She wanted to inform the country of what she had learned abroad—that birth control clinics offering personal instruction to women were needed.

This was a perfect moment to start on that mission. Invitations to address meetings had flooded in. Hardly taking time to rest, she set out that spring of 1916 on a cross-country speaking tour. She still feared to make a speech. Her knees would shake violently when she reached the platform, and she was almost sick until the moment she got on her feet. Her audiences expected a toughened campaigner. They were startled by the sweet, frail woman who stood before them in a bright dress with lace at her neck. Her voice rang out with clear silvery strength: "The first right of every child is to be wanted, to be desired, to be planned with an intensity of love that gives it its title to being."

Her tour opened in Pittsburgh and Cleveland, where she organized birth control leagues. In Chicago, although influential social workers had notified her they were "not interested" in birth control, fifteen hundred women from the stockyards district paid their twenty-five cents admission to the meeting. Her hosts in Minneapolis were afraid that the city would offer a poor audience. At meeting time only a dozen people were scattered in the hall. But as Margaret started to speak, hundreds poured in, and soon the hall was jammed with workers and farmers from the outlying districts who had not seen the notice of the meeting until the evening paper.

St. Paul, Milwaukee, Detroit—with thousands of women signing for new leagues. Often they came carrying little bouquets of wild flowers—daisies, Queen Anne's lace—which they shyly handed Margaret after the meeting, murmuring how grateful they were because her pamphlet had kept them "out of trouble."

Then St. Louis, and the first fireworks of the tour. Margaret's supporters had booked the Victoria Theater for May 21, and paid in advance. But when she arrived for the meeting, the theater doors were locked and the disappointed crowd jammed the street outside. The *Post-Dispatch* explained the next day that the manager had given in to "protests from Catholic priests and laymen." It was the first of a long series of extralegal attacks from the Roman Catholic hierarchy, whose religious position opposed the whole principle of birth control. (Fifty years later so many Catholic priests and laymen had come to support birth control for Catholics that most parishes throughout the country were sharply split on the issue.)

The leading papers in town complained about such attempts to throttle free speech and pointed out that it only set people to thinking and talking about Margaret's message who might otherwise never have heard of her. The Men's City Club promptly asked Margaret to speak, and she drew an even larger audience than had recently come to hear former President Theodore Roosevelt.

In Denver, Los Angeles, Oakland she continued to attract huge crowds. In Portland, Oregon, an auto mechanic made reprints of *Family Limitation* and started selling them to the audience. The police arrested him. When Margaret held another rally to protest it, this time distributing her pamphlet herself, she and four associates were arrested, too. They all refused bail and stayed in jail.

At the trial the next day all defendants were found guilty, and the men fined ten dollars, which the judge decreed need not be paid. The women were not even fined. A storm of protest letters whirled down upon the newspapers, and men picketed in the streets, carrying signs that read: POOR WOMEN ARE DENIED WHAT THE RICH POSSESS. The editorials all backed Margaret. Out of it came another league, a grand climax to a three-month tour that had made birth control the most hotly debated issue of the day.

She came back to New York, exhausted by the relentless pace of the tour and the emotional drain of thousands and thousands of women pleading for help. She took an apartment on Fourteenth Street, west of Seventh Avenue, her sister Ethel moving in just above her. At home there was no rest, either. Women knocked at her door at seven in the morning on their way to work, timidly asking for a few minutes of her time. Her phone rang day and night. Hundreds of letters poured in each week.

One day three women from Brownsville, a poor neighborhood in Brooklyn, came to call on her. Each was the mother of four or more children. Looking for the "secret" of birth control, they recited the misery of endless poverty Margaret had heard so often, and told of the constant fear of still another baby hanging over them.

What could she do for such women? She had

given them hope; she had pointed to a new way; and in *Family Limitation* she had tried to offer practical advice on contraception. But was that enough? How could women who hardly spoke English and who could not afford a doctor learn to use modern contraceptive methods? They needed instruction, training, and free devices like the diaphragm and the pessary. Most of all, they needed a free and open clinic right in their own neighborhood. Birth control clinics had to be brought directly to the people, a chain of them stretching all across the country.

The risks were tremendous. The costs she could not even estimate. The next mail brought a check for fifty dollars from a friend in Los Angeles. With that flash of intuition that so often guided Margaret, she decided then and there what she must do. She would use the money to pay the first month's rent for the first American clinic. And she would start it in the Brownsville section of Brooklyn.

11. A CLINIC AND A JAIL

Brownsville was the most thickly populated district in Brooklyn. It was a rainy October day when Margaret and Fania Mindell—a Chicago supporter who had come East to help—tramped the streets to find the right place to open a clinic. Thousands of bleak tenements leaned together in rows as far as their eyes could see, offering scant comfort to the Jewish and Italian families who overflowed every door and window. At 46 Amboy Street they rented two empty first-floor rooms for fifty dollars a month.

Since no doctor could be found with the courage to supervise the clinic, Margaret would use her Dutch training to give contraceptive information. Her sister Ethel (now Mrs. Byrne), a veteran nurse, would assist her.

The first step was to write the Brooklyn district attorney, announcing the opening of the clinic. They did not mean to keep their plans a secret. Without waiting for a reply—which never came—they painted the rooms a glossy white, hung new curtains, and put in desks, chairs and a stove. They printed five thousand leaflets in English, Yiddish, and Italian, which began:

MOTHERS!
Can you afford to have a large family?
Do you want any more children?
If not, why do you have them?

Then they went through the neighborhood day after day, slipping the leaflets under doors or stuffing them into mailboxes.

On October 16, 1916, they were ready. The early sun was brilliant, the air crisp, and Ethel, Fania, and Margaret nervous. Would anyone come? They made a last check of the clinic. The inner room was fitted out with models of birth control devices and charts describing how they were to be used. Here Margaret and Ethel would explain contraception to seven or eight women at a time. In the outer room Fania would distribute literature and take careful case histories to establish a scientific basis for studying the effects of birth control on the community.

They were stacking the registration cards on the desk when Fania called, "Come outside and look!" A line stretched almost to the corner—at least a hundred people, women with babies in their arms, women with young married daughters, a few men urging their wives. All day and evening they came. One hundred and forty were given instructions that first day, and dozens more on line had to return the next morning.

When the papers carried the news of the historic opening of the first birth control clinic in America, women began to arrive from as far away as Massachusetts, Connecticut, and Pennsylvania. The *Brooklyn Eagle* reported that one woman of thirty-five said: "I have seven children. Just now I am wondering how I am going to get shoes for them. My husband earns fifteen dollars a week when he works, and he is a good man to me. I don't know what we'd do if another baby came."

On the ninth day, while Margaret was out interviewing a doctor she hoped to get as medical director, a tall, severe woman calling herself Mrs. Whitehurst came to get contraceptives. Fania at once suspected she was a policewoman, but they took care of her like anyone else.

The next afternoon at four, while the line still stretched round the corner, Mrs. Whitehurst pushed her way into the clinic and approached Margaret.

"Mrs. Sanger?"

"Yes."

"I'm a police officer. You're under arrest."

Other officers barred the outside door and arrested Fania, too. Ethel was out at the moment and was arrested later. The police lined up the clinic's patients, many of them panicky and in tears, and took their names and addresses. Margaret assured the women that only the clinic's staff were under arrest, but it took half an hour to persuade the police to release the patients.

The police seized all the pamphlets, the contraceptive supplies, and even the hundreds of confidential case histories. An excited crowd milled in the street, and news photographers snapped pictures as the police hustled Margaret toward the patrol wagon. She refused to be shoved inside and walked the mile to court, flanked by policemen.

Her night in the Raymond Street jail was one she never forgot. The smell of the mattress sickened her. The blankets were stiff with dirt, and she wrapped herself in her coat instead. She used the one clean object in the cell, her towel, to hide her face and head from the roaches that crawled from the walls.

Released on bail the next afternoon, she returned at once to the clinic and announced it was open again. The waiting room quickly filled up with mothers. But the police were ready. This time they closed the clinic for good, forcing the landlord to evict her as a "public nuisance" despite the one-year lease.

As Margaret and Fania walked to the patrol wagon, the whole neighborhood stood by, strangely motionless, silent, stunned, as though the last straw of hope had been snatched away from them. Then just as the police were about to drive off, Margaret saw a woman wheeling a baby carriage come around the corner on her way to the clinic. She struggled through the crowd toward the wagon, holding out her arms and screaming, "Come back! Come back and save me!"

Out on bail again, Margaret realized that this Brownsville case was different from her challenge to the Comstock law. Now she was charged with violating Section 1142 of the state's penal code. It said that *no one* could give contraceptive information for *any* reason. But another law, Section 1145, said that doctors could give contraceptive information for the cure and prevention of disease. Lawyers told her that this had been designed to protect the man from diseases he might acquire through sexual contact. But why shouldn't the woman, too, be protected? Wasn't it just as important that her health be protected from the exhaustion and illness of endless childbearing?

This reasoning meant a new defense plan. Her Brownsville case would be fought on a line that would ask the courts to interpret the law more broadly than before. It would mean a long fight, for the case would certainly need to be appealed to higher courts, and it would require costly legal help. So Margaret turned now to some of the wealthy women who had just joined the movement—women like Mrs. George Rublee, Mrs. J. Borden Harriman, Mrs. Charles Tiffany. They organized a "Committee of 100," which drew the support of many distinguished leaders of public opinion.

To handle her case she secured a brilliant young lawyer, Jonah J. Goldstein. After many postponements the trial opened on January 8, 1917. The courtroom was filled with women from Brownsville and the Committee of 100. Although Margaret insisted that she and Ethel should be tried together, her sister's case was called first. Ethel testified that, of course, she had prescribed birth control methods. She denied that the ten-cent registration fee made the clinic into a business. And it was ridiculous to say that the clinic was "intended to do away with the Jews," as some had charged.

Goldstein was allowed only fifteen minutes for his arguments against the constitutionality of Section 1142. The purpose of the law, he said, was to force people to have larger families. But what if there were a similar law to punish a bachelor over thirty who did not marry and raise a family? Or to punish a married couple who had purposely avoided having children? Would this not be a crippling of the personal liberty guaranteed us all by the Constitution?

The judge did not see it that way. He ruled the law was constitutional and sentenced Ethel to thirty days in the workhouse on Blackwell's Island in the East River. Ethel immediately told the press, "I shall go on a hunger strike. I shall die, if need be, for the cause."

Her hope was that word of the hunger strike

would be considered news for the front page and rally women everywhere behind the movement. The warden's wife could not stand to see her not eating and tried to tempt Ethel with the odor of bacon and eggs. She begged her prisoner to eat: "I'll give you the food secretly. Nobody will know you've taken a bite."

"I'd know," Ethel replied.

Within a few days Ethel's hunger strike was competing with the war news from Europe for the headlines. "It will be hard to make the youth of 1967 believe that in 1917 a woman was imprisoned for doing what Mrs. Byrne did," wrote Franklin P. Adams, the widely read columnist.

After Ethel had gone 103 hours without food or water, the Commissioner of Correction ordered her to be fed by force. No one had ever done this to a woman in America before. They wound Ethel tightly in a blanket to prevent a struggle and, with a tube, forced down her throat a mixture of milk, eggs, and brandy.

From Goldstein—the only person allowed to visit Ethel—Margaret learned that her sister's health was cracking. Then a reporter managed a secret interview with Ethel and told Margaret her sister's condition was rapidly getting worse. With Mrs. Amos Pinchot, head of the Committee of 100 and a friend of Governor Charles Whitman of New York, Margaret caught the next train to Albany. The governor was sympathetic, but refused to grant a pardon unless Ethel promised not to break the law again. With a pass from the governor, the two women rushed to the prison. Ethel, starved almost to skin and bones, was lying on her cot, breathing feebly; she did not even move at the sound of her name. Her eyes were sunken, her voice hardly a whisper. "I must go away, I must go away," she kept repeating.

Nothing mattered now to Margaret but her sister's life. She would have to take the responsibility for Ethel's future conduct. She immediately telegraphed the governor, guaranteeing that her sister would take no part in the birth control movement while her case was being appealed through the courts.

An hour later the governor signed the pardon. Ethel was carried on a stretcher to an ambulance that took her to Margaret's apartment. It was two weeks before she completely regained her health. Her courage had given a tremendous lift to the movement, demonstrating for the first time in America that a woman was willing to risk her life to win all women the right of choice in child-bearing.

Margaret's trial opened on January 29 in the same bare Brooklyn courtroom where Ethel had been convicted. With Margaret's history of tuberculosis, Goldstein was determined she should not risk jail. The national sympathy aroused by Ethel's hunger strike made him certain he could get a suspended sentence. But Margaret told him flatly, "No compromise!"

In the front rows of the court sat the society women newly won to the cause and behind them the Brownsville mothers, who brought babies, spare diapers, and food. The district attorney had subpoenaed thirty of the clinic patients, and one after another he called them to the stand to testify to what was admitted: that Margaret had given them advice on contraceptives. They praised Margaret for helping them, not realizing this was evidence to be used against her. Then Goldstein called them back to the stand.

"How many children do you have?"

"Eight, and three that didn't live," said the first.

"Seven living and two dead," said the next.

"Nine living and one dead," said the third.

And so the answers went, hour after hour. A record of miscarriages and sickness and poverty and hunger and despair. It was a pattern of lives twisted and tortured by law that had no feeling for humanity.

The panel of three judges was obviously moved. Goldstein made clear that his real aim was to appeal the case to the Supreme Court. He hoped the judges would not punish Margaret heavily while the long-range fight continued. But the court demanded that in return for leniency she must publicly declare that she would not violate the law.

Margaret answered that she was willing not to violate Section 1142—pending the appeal.

"The appeal has nothing to do with it," the court insisted. "What's your answer, Mrs. Sanger —is it yes or no?"

There was a terrible silence in the courtroom. Everyone stared at Margaret, saw her slight body stiffen, her face tighten. Then, in a quiet voice, she said: "I cannot promise to obey a law I do not respect."

Every woman in the room shouted and clapped as the court gaveled for silence. When order was restored, the sentence was announced: Margaret would be confined to the workhouse for thirty days. A woman's voice in the rear cried, "Shame!" And it was all over.

Margaret was taken to another room for finger-printing. She refused to allow it; it would be admitting that opening a birth control clinic was the same as committing a crime. She was taken in a patrol wagon to the Raymond Street jail, and ordered to prepare for a medical examination. Again she decided that any act putting her on the same level as a criminal must be resisted. The matron threatened to use force, but a higher official vetoed it. She was locked up for the night and taken the next day to the Kings County prison.

Within a week Margaret got to know the women in her cell block. They were mostly drug addicts, prostitutes, shoplifters, thieves. She wondered if there was any connection between crime and large families, and persuaded the warden to let her study the records. In her own corridor of thirty-seven women she learned that seven brothers and sisters was the average number in each family. Ten of the women were illiterate, and she gave them lessons in reading and writing, using the letters they received and wanted to send.

Why not educate them on birth control, too, she thought. Most of the women liked the idea. The matron scoffed at it, but with Margaret's persistence, and popularity among the prisoners, she was finally allowed to start a series of daily lectures.

Letters from everywhere reached her in jail, among them several from the famous Socialist leader, Eugene Debs, then fighting to rally workers to resist American involvement in the European war. "You are being tried in every fiber," he wrote Margaret, "but you have the stuff that stands and you are bound to win. Oh, for a million women rebels to catch the clarion cry of Margaret Sanger and proclaim the glad tidings of woman's coming freedom throughout the world!"

March 6, the day of her release, drew close. She was treated well till then, but the last day was terrible. The warden insisted on taking her fingerprints, and two keepers tried to force her fingers down on the ink pad. One held her while the other wrenched her arms into position, but she struggled so hard they could not make her fingers touch the pad. After two hours, weak and bruised, she was let go on order from police headquarters.

The winter morning was bitterly cold. But freedom made her feel warm inside. She stepped through the big metal doorway into the gray day. Out front to celebrate her "coming out" were many of her old friends. When they saw the slim redheaded figure emerge they lifted their voices in the revolutionary "Marseillaise." Margaret joined in, tears filming her eyes, and then, floating through the windows of the cells high above, came the voices of her new friends singing with her the triumphant words, "Ye sons of freedom wake to glory!"

The legal fight continued, appeals moving from one court to the next. On January 8, 1918, Judge Frederick E. Crane of the New York Court of Appeals issued a crucial decision. Although he upheld Margaret's conviction, he defined the meaning of Section 1145 so broadly that it changed the whole application of the law from then on.

Before, under this section, doctors could prescribe contraceptive devices to prevent "disease" —which had been taken to mean syphilis and gonorrhea. In other words, a doctor could prescribe a male sheath to protect a man from catching a venereal disease.

Now, under the judge's new liberal interpretation, the word "disease" must mean what the dictionary said—any sickness or disorder or any change in the functions of the body that might affect health. Section 1145, said Judge Crane, now permitted doctors to give birth control advice to a married woman in order to protect her health.

At last the sword over every doctor's head had been removed. Margaret's challenge to the law in Brownsville had opened the way to establish birth control clinics.

12. HARD YEARS

These were hard years for Margaret. It was natural for organizers to be on the payroll of the unions or social movements they devoted themselves to. But Margaret would never accept a salary. She scraped along on her lecture fees and magazine articles, and later on the sale of her books. Food and rent were almost all she could pay for; there was little left for clothing. Sometimes when she was to appear before a distinguished audience a friend would lend her a dress for the evening and then gently insist she keep it for herself. The room on Fourteenth Street, worn and shabby, offered scant comfort. A few pieces of furniture and an old rug did little to cheer it. She tried to dress it up with yellow curtains, but the room was always witness to the loneliness and poverty that came from complete dedication to the movement.

Since 1914 when she had separated from Bill Sanger, no one had ever taken his place. In these years she came together with men only as part of her work, though they may have tried to make the relationship more personal. A newspaperman who helped Margaret prepare one of her books wrote her that "these two weeks were the happiest, the most inspiring I have ever known. . . . I have loved you beyond my power to understand it."

She made her admirers realize that the movement always came first. It was harsh on herself and on them, but she had to have it that way. "I didn't have time to waste on people unless they would do something to help forward the movement," she said.

In the little time left for her personal life, she put her sons first. She wanted to spend every spare moment with Stuart and Grant, who were away at school first on Long Island and then in New Jersey. If she had kept the boys with her, they would have been alone most of the time, while at boarding school they got excellent teaching and constant care. But the separation often became so painful to her she would suddenly jump on a train to see them if only for a few minutes.

The role of crusader's son was not easy for the boys. The schools helped give them the stability and discipline they needed. Since she could not afford their cost by herself, it was lucky that her sisters Nan and Mary, and Bill Sanger, too, were able to contribute to the tuition. What Margaret wanted badly was a place where she could spend whole summers with the boys. Her friend John Reed made it possible when he was suddenly assigned to cover the outbreak of the Russian Revolution. He offered his cottage at Truro on Cape Cod, and with a thousand-dollar windfall from a lecture series in Chicago, she was able to make the down payment. She and the boys spent many wonderful summer weekends together, but never the long months she hoped for.

Much of Margaret's energy was now poured into the *Birth Control Review*. Founded in February 1917, it remained the voice of the movement for almost a quarter of a century. Its pages carried the most advanced thinking on the scientific aspects of the population problem. Experts, such as H. G. Wells, Havelock Ellis, and Professor Henry Pratt Fairchild of New York University, wrote for it. Editing it was job enough; on top of that she scurried everywhere to find the money to meet the printing bills. Soon she realized she had to set up a permanent publishing company to give the magazine a firm base. She enlisted Mrs. Rublee and other wealthy friends of the Committee of 100 to buy shares and help with circulation and fund raising.

For the first time now Margaret had an office of

her own—two small rooms at 104 Fifth Avenue with only the words "Birth Control" on the door. Her secretary was a slight, dark-haired girl, Anna Lipschiz, fresh from high school. She, too, was from a large family—seven children—and she was on fire for the cause. She insisted on taking only a tiny salary and often waited weeks for it without complaint. Margaret had the same effect on everyone. Volunteers rushed in and out, eager to do the work of freeing women from the bonds of unwanted births.

"It was like a religious crusade," Anna recalled. "Through it Mrs. Sanger moved confidently, giving us all some added strength that would make us work thirteen hours that day when we were sure we couldn't last ten."

The most valuable new recruit was Kitty Marion. She had run away from her home in Germany as a girl, gone on the London music hall stage, then joined the women's crusade for the right to vote. She arrived here from England with extraordinary credentials—she had been jailed seven times, survived four hunger strikes, and endured scores of forced feedings. Kitty was a believer in direct action, in confrontation with the enemy. Even in jail she could not be passive. Once she set fire to her cell, and another time she escaped from a nursing home where the police had confined her. Charged with hurling a bag of flour at the prime minister, she replied, "It's a lie! I have never in my life thrown anything so soft as a bag of flour!"

To the birth control movement she brought a

new vitality and a new technique—the sale of the *Review* on street corners. Her sturdy figure, blonde hair, and blue eyes were soon familiar opposite Grand Central Terminal, at Times Square, and near Macy's. Often she sold a thousand copies a month, despite all kinds of abuse from boys, old ladies, and the police.

Another new figure in the movement, the first really professional organizer and supervisor of the Fifth Avenue office, was Dr. Frederick Blossom. He had met Margaret in Cleveland on her 1916 spring tour. Convinced of the importance of birth control, he decided to join the New York office for six months. He had broad experience in raising money for Cleveland charities, and his charm enabled him to attract volunteers. A tireless worker, he developed an effective system for answering the heavy mail and took over the details of scheduling lectures and running the New York Birth Control League.

Although Margaret was delighted to have the burdensome details taken off her hands, she and Blossom soon clashed. The first issue was the war in Europe. A staunch pacifist who favored neither the Allies nor the Germans, Margaret opposed United States intervention. Blossom strongly favored the French and tried to swing the *Review*'s editorial policy behind the Allies. But beyond this, Blossom's ambitions soon made him think he could take over leadership of the birth control movement and use Margaret simply as an inspirational speechmaker.

The conflict came into the open one May morning, when Margaret arrived at the office to find that Blossom had removed all the files, records, checks, and furniture. Only a telephone was left. Margaret and Anna at once put in a few pieces of secondhand furniture and went on working despite the crippling loss. It was a low point for the movement. The need to keep going made an enormous demand upon her. She believed "faith could bring anything to realization." She looked upon this bleak time calmly; the roots she had put down were deep and growing, though little might yet be seen upon the surface. Her belief in herself powered the frail machine of her body to dictate scores of letters, to interview a dozen people, to attend a meeting, to speak at a forum, all in one working day. Nevertheless, toward the end of the year she was so worn by the running fight with Blossom and the struggle to keep the movement afloat that she said she felt like hiding in some cave where she could spend the rest of her life laughing at the world.

Instead, with an advance from a publisher, she buried herself for a few months with Grant in a beach house at Coronado. There in the California sun she wrote the first draft of her book, *Woman and the New Race.* She reworked much of it the following year. Published in 1920, it swiftly became the cornerstone of the movement, selling a quarter of a million copies here and many thousands abroad.

In the winter of 1920 Margaret sailed for

Europe again. She had always been looking for new, improved methods of contraception—something simpler, safer, cheaper. From Havelock Ellis she heard about a new chemical contraceptive, a jelly made in Germany that he considered an important advance. She arrived to find Germany starving, broken by its defeat in the war. The streets of Berlin were dark, silent, the shop windows bare. Few people were about, and they moved heavily, never smiling. In the fields she saw women reduced to animals, pulling plows in place of draft horses, hungry children were everywhere. "God, what pinched, empty little faces," she wrote. Population and war—wasn't there a link? She was convinced that Germany's rapid population increase from 40 to 70 million in recent decades had been one of the leading causes of her military gamble. When Margaret wanted to discuss birth control with German doctors, she heard them say they looked upon the woman as breeder for the male; they did not want to put the decision for birth in her hands. The male must dominate in this as in all matters that concerned the power of the state and the army. To Margaret it was more proof of the connection between population and war—a theme that was to run through her thinking from then on.

She followed clues from Berlin to Dresden to Munich and finally found the chemists, a father and son, at Friedrichshafen on Lake Constance. A small man, his coat patched, his hair uncut, met her at the station, carrying a bunch of wild flowers wrapped in a newspaper. Her questions came fast. Was he making the chemical jelly? Yes, in a small factory, a family operation. Could they go there? Well, they didn't like to have visitors. Besides, they should have coffee first. He kept her talking for hours, until she realized he feared she might steal the formula. But wait, he had a sister in New York who could act as the firm's agent. Why couldn't Margaret buy the jelly from her? They discussed price. And Margaret signed an agreement in the café.

Before leaving, however, she arranged to get some samples so that the formula's value could be tested in New York. There it proved not to be "a magic solution." It was, also, expensive and difficult to import. But American chemists set about improving it. Eventually the jelly became the basis of many chemical contraceptives prescribed by clinics.

Margaret stopped in London on the way home, exhausted and haunted by what she had seen in Germany. Resting only briefly, she gave a series of thirty lectures to workers' wives, arranged by Dr. Alice Vickery. Almost daily she went to a different part of London—dockyards, slums, market-places—speaking and holding demonstration clinics. Then on to Scotland for more.

Back in London, Havelock Ellis introduced her to friends at a country place in Sussex. Wantley was a beautiful stone house with oak beams and huge fireplaces, owned once by Shelley's father and now by Hugh de Sélincourt, a poet and novelist. The Wantley circle, which included Ellis and H. G. Wells, was a marvelous refuge for Margaret.

The days were filled with music, reading, walks on the moors. At night they sat around the fire, the conversation flowing from some of the most brilliant minds in England. To Wantley she brought a special quality of love. She was the ideal writers wrote about, the ideal made real, the woman rebel who had challenged the world yet retained all the sweetness of the feminine spirit.

From Wantley she went to stay with H. G. Wells and his wife, Jane. Their estate in Essex was a redbrick Tudor house with sweeping lawns and soaring blue cedars. Here amidst crowds of visitors, such as Bernard Shaw and Bertrand Russell, the weekends were like fantastic dreams for a woman whose horizon had once been limited to Corning, New York. Wells, devoted to the new freedom for women, loved Margaret's daring. She was the symbol who acted out what he had put on paper. Although he pursued her in London and later in New York, neither he nor anyone else she then knew was to carry her off. Her divorce from Bill Sanger became final in October 1920, but she still avoided any permanent tie with a man. Fascinating as were many of the men she met, none could hold her. Strangely enough, the man she would marry—and the time was closer than she realized—would be as different from Ellis and Wells and the rest of their circle as if he had come from another world.

13. BIRTH CONTROL: IS IT MORAL?

All that Sunday afternoon Margaret was troubled. She had a strange feeling something was going wrong. She couldn't get her brain to focus on the speech she had to make in a few hours. Yet up to now everything had seemed to be going well. With a year's hard work she had won support from major women's groups. Now the Birth Control League was able to hold the First National Birth Control Conference.

Tonight the conference would end with an open meeting on the question, "Birth Control: Is It Moral?" Town Hall had been reserved and paid for three weeks earlier. Harold Cox, a former

member of Parliament and one of England's bes
orators, had arrived from London to be the fea
tured speaker. Everything was arranged, but stil
Margaret felt strangely nervous and anxious. Sh
dined early with Mrs. Rublee and Cox, and ther
took a taxi to Town Hall. When they reache
Forty-third Street, thousands of people stoo
jammed in front of the building. This is grea
Margaret thought, an overflow meeting!

They got out of the cab and pushed their wa
to the door. But two policemen barred the en
trance. "There's not going to be any meeting to
night," they announced.

"But who stopped it?" Margaret asked. "We'r
the speakers!"

The police could give no answer. Margare
crossed the street to a phone booth and called po
lice headquarters. They had no orders to stop th
meeting, but could not tell her how to reach th
commissioner.

Margaret knew she had to get inside. Someon
had to take command. Health officials, doctor:
lawyers, milled around on the sidewalk, angr
puzzled, wondering what was going on. She sa
someone slipping out of a side door, and befor
she could be stopped, Margaret darted under a
officer's arm and through the door, disappearin
into the crowd inside. She wormed her way to th
foot of the stage. Another policeman was blockin
the steps, but suddenly a man lifted her and swun
her up onto the stage. Leaping up beside her, h
shouted, "Here she is! Here's Mrs. Sanger!"

"Don't leave! Don't leave!" Margaret cried to the audience. "We're going to hold the meeting!"

The hall thundered with applause, and people moved back to their seats. At this point, one reporter said, there were over five thousand people in the street outside, struggling to get into Town Hall.

While people were being seated, Anne Kennedy, an associate, told Margaret what had happened. At eight o'clock, with the opening a half hour away and the hall half filled, Captain Donohue of the local precinct had come to the platform with Monsignor Dineen, secretary to Archbishop Patrick J. Hayes of the New York Roman Catholic archdiocese. "The meeting must be closed," the monsignor said. "Why?" asked Mrs. Kennedy. "An indecent, immoral subject is to be discussed," he replied.

What right had the church to interfere? Monsignor Dineen turned to the police captain. "The meeting must be closed," Donohue echoed.

Margaret was angrily determined the meeting must go on. It was one thing to have a meeting stopped by a misguided or ignorant policeman. But it was a far more serious act—a violation of the constitutional right of free speech and assembly —to have a public meeting stopped by a high dignitary of the Roman Catholic Church.

Stepping to the front of the platform and raising her hand, Margaret cried, "Ladies and gentlemen! You have all seen—"

Two officers stepped forward and stopped her

from speaking. The audience hissed and booed. "Where's your warrant?" Margaret demanded. "What's the charge?"

Harold Cox, a tall, white-haired elder statesman of Parliament, stepped to the front and said, "I have come from across the Atlantic—" He got no further. Another policeman pulled him back to his seat.

Miss Mary Winsor, president of the Pennsylvania Equal Suffrage Association, stood up to speak. She, too, was stopped. Again and again, Margaret, Cox, and other speakers tried to say something and were interrupted by the police while the audience roared its protest.

A second squad of police had now entered the hall. At the back of the stage Monsignor Dineen continued to give instructions to Captain Donohue through police messengers. Now he gave the final command. The captain ordered his men to arrest Margaret. Miss Winsor started to speak again. She, too, was arrested. Yet no law had been broken at this legally authorized meeting—except by the police. As Mrs. Rublee and the other women crowded around, they, too, were arrested.

The audience started to sing "My country, 'tis of thee" as the police herded Margaret and the others out of the hall and toward the patrol wagon. They refused to board it, and insisted on walking to the station house. Lines of police surrounded them, but the crowd pressed close, now singing, now hissing. Thousands escorted the prisoners all the way to the station.

At night court the magistrate quickly released Margaret and the others, ordering them to appear the next morning. Meanwhile, a *New York Times* reporter finally reached Monsignor Dineen by telephone at his office in St. Patrick's Cathedral.

"Yes," said the monsignor, "I ordered the meeting to be closed."

In court the next day the magistrate waited an hour for Captain Donohue to appear with the charges. He never showed up. The district attorney admitted there was no evidence of illegality. The case was dismissed.

But not ended. Almost every major New York paper attacked the church and the police in their editorials. "If people cannot come together in a perfectly orderly and open way to debate whether or not a matter is moral," the *Post* said, "then our boasted freedom of speech is a mockery."

Margaret quickly turned the blunder of the church and the police into an important victory with press and public. The archbishop, intent on crushing the birth control movement, had ignored the Bill of Rights. Margaret cleverly seized the broader issue. She fought back as the defender of free speech and assembly. This approach brought hundreds of headlines and favorable editorials in the next few days, many in conservative papers that had never been friendly to birth control.

Then she announced that the disrupted meeting would be held again the following Friday. This time the Park Theater at Columbus Circle was booked. By eight o'clock that evening thousands were packed so tight in the street outside the theater that only one door could be opened. Every seat was taken in minutes. Some of the disappointed tried to get in by climbing the fire escapes.

Refusing to let the Town Hall closing disappear from the headlines, Margaret announced she would "take this case to the highest courts, if necessary, to preclude the possibility of it ever happening again." When twenty-eight prominent New Yorkers signed an open letter demanding Captain Donohue's punishment, the police commissioner was finally forced to order an investigation.

The hearings were a farce. Most of the time was spent questioning Margaret and others not about Town Hall but about the Brownsville clinic and birth control. Again the press attacked the police, this time for the foolish way they were carrying out the inquiry. Another group of business and civic leaders issued an open letter to the mayor, stating: "The action of the Police Department constitutes such a willful violation of the right of free speech as to cause grave alarm to the citizens of New York."

The mayor then ordered a second investigation of his previous investigation! Again the testimony showed that orders to close the Town Hall meeting had come from police headquarters.

From whom at headquarters?

Why, Police Captain Donohue said, it was just the phone operator.

Every official was keeping his mouth tightly

shut. As the investigation dragged on month after month, the public saw there was no intention of placing the blame where it belonged. Monsignor Dineen was never criticized. No report was ever issued. No one in the police was ever punished. And some time later, Donohue was promoted to the rank of inspector and then quietly retired.

Margaret failed to win justice this time, but she did succeed in winning public opinion. Throughout the country the church's attempt to curb constitutional liberties was opposed. The birth control movement had not been turned back.

14. A NEW KIND OF MARRIAGE

What would an imaginary portrait of the man least likely to attract Margaret's attention have looked like? President of an oil company? Pillar of the Episcopal church? Member of the Union League Club? J. Noah Slee—even the name seems made up!—was all three. This tall, ruddy-faced man who looked like a country squire appears in Margaret's history for the first time in the spring of 1921. She mentions him in a letter to Mrs. Rublee, telling her of the prosperous businessman who was flying over from Paris to spend a day with her in London.

Taken by a friend to one of Margaret's meetings the winter before, Slee was at first divided in his feelings. He admired Margaret greatly (later he said he knew he had to win her the minute they met) but was wary of the birth control movement. His admiration gradually won out. Soon he was attending every meeting and sending large bouquets of roses to Margaret's office.

They were worlds apart at the start of their friendship. An imposing figure with his white hair and bushy black eyebrows, Slee had the formal manner of an aristocrat. His old-world air was heightened by the rimless glasses that he wore attached by a black band to a dapper waistcoat trimmed with piping. His eyes were dark and often stern. He had been brought up on the Bible, read it to his children every Sunday, and said grace at every meal. At St. George's Church, where the J. P. Morgans and their friends worshipped, Slee had been the superintendent of the Sunday school for twenty-five years. "I nearly fainted when he told me that," Margaret said.

But there was no resisting his smile, the radiant kindness, the touches of tenderness. Because of an unhappy marriage, he had buried his feelings while he gave all his time to his business. Now under Margaret's gaiety he began to unfold. He even learned to dance when she casually mentioned she liked to.

The influence was two-way. She changed, too, under the example of this careful businessman, who despite great wealth still kept a pocket notebook of his daily expenses. Noting she had trou-

ble keeping her appointments, he asked her what
kind of watch she used. She admitted she didn't
own one, but simply glanced out the office window at the clock across the street. Shocked, he
sent her a fine watch the next day, and soon Margaret was as devoted to split-second accuracy as
Slee.

But his greatest effect was on the movement itself. One morning he wandered into her office and
saw the mailbags—thousands of letters that came
in constantly from women all over the country.
But how slowly and inefficiently the mail was being handled! He reorganized the department at
once, bought a mechanical letter opener, a date
stamper, new typewriters, and set up a new fil-
ing system. Before long he was the one man she
could always rely on, the man who gave her backing in every crisis. He became the chief financial
resource, too, gradually moving toward the center of her projects.

In the early twenties, Margaret kept saying in
her speeches and articles that the greatest threat
to the peace of the world would come from the
expanding population of Asia. Her chance to visit
the Far East came in the spring of 1922. The
Kaizo publishing group invited her to make a
lecture tour of Japan.

Margaret knew that Japan's population had
soared to 33,000,000 people during the industrial
revolution of the last century and had almost
doubled since 1872. Over 2600 Japanese had to
live off each square mile of agricultural land com-

pared with 466 in England. Squeezed into a few tiny islands, these new millions could be the spark to set off a new war, Margaret predicted—a prediction that would come true in Japan's invasion of Manchuria and then in her attack on Pearl Harbor.

Margaret decided to take along Grant, then thirteen. Stuart, a stocky, handsome youth of eighteen, who was captain of the football team at Peddie and preparing for Yale, could look after himself. The tireless Mr. Slee went to San Francisco to see them off on the ship. At the last moment he decided to book passage, too. In those two weeks at sea nothing could interfere with his courtship.

Again Margaret found barriers in her path. The birth control movement was making rapid strides in Japan. The government, dominated by militarists, was using a new "Dangerous Thought Law" to suppress progressive ideas. They feared her influence on Japanese youth. Her request for visas was refused, and she had to get last-minute visas from China in order to sail. Aboard ship she continued to press for Japanese visas through cablegrams.

When the ship stopped at Hawaii, Margaret lectured to a large crowd, and two Japanese reporters cabled enthusiastic reports to their home papers. By the time she reached Tokyo, her coming had been front-page news for two weeks. "Since the coming of Commodore Perry," wrote Baroness Ishimoto, a young progressive leader, "no American had created a greater sensation in the land of the Mikado than Margaret Sanger."

After the ship reached Tokyo, seventy newsmen tried to crowd into Margaret's cabin. Then government officials interviewed her for hours as she continued the battle for entry. Finally they agreed to admit her if she did not lecture publicly on the war-and-population theme. The Kaizo people kept up pressure, and in a few days Margaret was told that the Minister of Home Affairs had reversed his stand. She would be allowed to speak on population control.

She set off on a hectic two-week lecture program, giving ten talks in the second week alone. "I have never spoken with greater freedom," she wrote home, "and I have never had a more appreciative audience."

Her impact on Japan can be measured by the five hundred newspaper articles written about her tour. In the following month 81 out of 108 monthly magazines carried features on birth control. "She appeared like a comet," Baroness Ishimoto wrote, "and left such a vivid and long-enduring impression on the Japanese mind that there is no possibility of reckoning the true value of her visit."

China was next. There she was to be the guest of Dr. Hu Shih, the noted writer and scholar. Educated at Cornell and Columbia, he was considered the father of the Chinese literary renaissance. Slee, who had been doing business in Japan, decided to go with her and Grant.

The poverty she saw in the China of the twenties, the mass breeding, the cheapness of life which had led Chinese women for centuries to limit their families by drowning or suffocating unwanted babies, overwhelmed Margaret. At a cotton mill on the Yangtze River she saw hundreds of girls under eight working ten-hour days for a nickel a day. The mothers in the mill kept their infants in baskets beside the machines. Homeless women gave birth to children in the streets, with no one paying attention. Although she had planned no lectures in China, she could not be silent in the face of this misery. She agreed to make a few speeches. In Peking and again in Shanghai she stressed that China with its starving millions was "the best argument in the world for birth control." Many of the papers supported her but said it would be a hard campaign: "So hard," wrote one, "that if it were won, the education of the rest of the world would be a simple matter."

Then the three of them traveled by boat to Port Said and on to Cairo, where Grant came down with dysentery. It was a serious case. His temperature rose to 104 degrees and stayed there despite the efforts of the doctors. As Margaret sat by his bed day and night, all the terrible moments of Peggy's last illness rose to haunt her. On the fourth day, with Grant's temperature still high, Margaret decided to act herself. Ordering a bucket of ice, she sponged him down with cold water and lowered his temperature to normal in a few hours. Slee, who had grown very fond of him, now took command and suggested he take Grant to Switzerland for a few weeks where the boy could recover his strength.

In London a month later, Slee insisted that Margaret must now finally marry him. But she still wanted time to think. She went to see Havelock Ellis. All these years they had written to each other every week. The link between them had constantly grown stronger. But a permanent relationship was no more possible now than it had been earlier. Ellis needed someone willing to fit neatly into his own studies and writing, into his need for a quiet, untroubled home. That was no life for Margaret, not while the movement swept her on with its unending demands.

If she could not marry a philosopher and poet, how then could she accept Slee? The simple fact was that he was ready to take Margaret on her own terms. With his wealth, his social standing, his importance in the business world, he found he could not do without a woman who was a world away from all this. She wanted complete personal independence and the right to devote herself to the birth control movement. And he agreed to those conditions.

She would be known as Margaret Sanger in the movement, as Mrs. Slee only at social affairs. They would live in the same house—but in separate apartments. She had her own group of friends—intellectuals, artists, writers—who would probably not interest him. He had his own business circle and could entertain them separately if he liked. So they would each keep the individual pattern of their lives.

She knew that once Slee had accepted her terms, he would never go back on his word. "I made it terribly hard for him," she admitted later. "I threw every obstacle in his path." Later there were times when he found their agreement hard to take and almost rebelled.

Why did he agree to this arrangement? Because he considered her the most beautiful and fascinating woman he had ever known. And he became increasingly proud of the movement she led. She was "the greatest adventure of my life," he said once.

They were married in London before a justice of the peace. When they returned to New York, they took two apartments at 39 Fifth Avenue, one of the handsome new buildings springing up north of Washington Square, just a few blocks from Margaret's office. Then they built a luxurious home at Fishkill on the Hudson. The main house was planned by Margaret. Of local fieldstone, it sat almost at the edge of a lake surrounded by willows. It had three stories under its slanting slate roof. On the main floor was a huge living room, a library, dining room, and breakfast room. Above were four master bedrooms and the servants' rooms. At the far corner of the lake was a six-room gardener's cottage.

They kept a stable of horses and rode through the surrounding hills almost every morning before breakfast. "Willow Lake," as they called it, was made for entertaining. On weekends there was open house for swarms of Stuart's and Grant's young friends.

Despite a staff of servants, Margaret liked to do much of the cooking for guests herself. Their parties were often in costume. The evenings were climaxed with dancing on the grass and swimming in the lake, two things Margaret loved.

Her special pride was the gardens—especially the groves of lilac bushes that surrounded and hid her private study called "Tree Tops." Here she came to work and write. Yet even in summer she took the train almost daily to her office in New York.

Not everything went smoothly between Margaret and her husband. At first he felt Margaret should spend more time at their beautiful country home than at her work. But Slee himself was drawn more and more deeply into the movement, even taking on official duties. He gave large sums of money year after year. Inevitably people said Slee's wealth was the reason for Margaret's marriage. But all the evidence indicates she loved him for his great, gentle heart, and needed the warmth, the security, the confidence, the stability, he offered.

Gruff on the outside, he softened instantly to the appeal of a personal cause. He gave thousands of dollars yearly to young singers and artists to continue their studies. But the most important gift of all he made on his next trip to

London with Margaret. It was the occasion of Havelock Ellis's sixty-ninth birthday. Ellis had received little reward for a lifetime of brilliant research and writing. He was still living in his little flat and supporting two maiden sisters.

Margaret and her husband decided the birthday was a perfect moment for a final proof of their love and appreciation. But it had to be done subtly so as not to offend him. Their mutual friend, Hugh de Sélincourt, handled the details, buying a house where Ellis could live for the rest of his life and paying a salary to a friend so that she could give up teaching and devote her full time to Ellis's work and keeping house for him.

Ellis chose a house at Herne Hill, and when De Sélincourt went out to visit him there, he wrote to Margaret and Slee: "You have made Havelock ten years younger. I wish I could make you feel every ripple of delight that lovely action of yours is bringing and will continue to bring."

15. TEN THOUSAND
CRIES FOR HELP

Day after day the letters piled up in her office:

The doctor said when the last one was born
that I should not have any more children—I
have seven already—but when I asked him
what I could do, he simply said nothing. I
would rather die than have any more. . . .
Please, dear Mrs. Sanger will you tell me
what to do?

I have been married ten years and I have
had six children, and two are dead, one mis-
carriage and one still born. Oh God, I

wouldn't want any more....

The letters came from all over the country, ten thousand a month now, the voices of mothers, intimate, heartrending, pleading for help:

> I have went to the doctors and had illegal operations performed until I couldn't afford it any longer and then tried doing it myself until I'm afraid I'll have myself ruined. I think I will lose my mind....

And the women themselves came, often making long trips in the hope that a few minutes with Mrs. Sanger would save them from another unwanted pregnancy.

The number of requests for help had grown so large that the Birth Control League assigned three secretaries to answering them. Each mother was sent a copy of *Family Limitation*. As Margaret also collected a file of doctors friendly to birth control, she would send each woman the name of a doctor nearest her. But in some parts of the country "nearest" meant a trip of hundreds of miles.

No, this couldn't be the answer. It wasn't enough. This was only a stopgap measure. Ever since that day in 1916 when the police had closed the Brownsville clinic, Margaret had been planning for a better medical center, a research agency that would be run completely by doctors, constantly studying contraceptive methods and developing new and better ones. The Brownsville clinic in its short life had mainly served to test the law. But with Judge Crane's decision of 1918, a reasonable amount of protection for the medical profession had been won.

Now, after years of public education, Margaret was convinced the time was ripe for a clinical research bureau that would be the backbone of the movement. She hoped it would become the model for a chain of hundreds of clinics from coast to coast. She had thought it out carefully. She saw the clinic as a part of the public health system, doing its share in providing total health care for the family. And it would also be a laboratory for human research, making a scientific study of the patients it cared for, so that research in the birth control field could keep moving forward.

Since the bureau would surely be attacked, she wanted to keep it separate from the American Birth Control League. She organized a board for it with such prominent physicians and scientists as Dr. C. C. Little, president of the University of Michigan; Professor Raymond Pearl, the sociologist; and Dr. Adolph Myer, the Johns Hopkins psychiatrist.

It took weeks to raise the money needed to open the bureau and assure the salary of a medical director, and months more to find a doctor willing to take the risks of this crucial job. Despite the Crane decision, it was yet to be proved that the courts would interpret the law to cover a doctor practicing in a birth control clinic. Margaret put the issue this way: "For one doctor to stand up and assert her right under this legal opinion would give tremendous impetus and encouragement to thousands of other doctors throughout the country to do likewise."

Finally Margaret had a medical director. In January 1923 the Clinical Research Bureau opened in two rooms at the same Fifth Avenue address where the league was. The plan was not to publicize the bureau; the patients would be referred to it from among the women who came to the league for help.

The file cards Margaret designed for the patients showed what her goal was. She wanted to investigate the whole area of sex knowledge in marriage—a pioneering step she took long before the studies of Dr. Alfred Kinsey at the University of Indiana. There was basic information on national origin, husband's and wife's occupation and income, religion, number of children, miscarriages, stillbirths, and abortions. Beyond this, the interviewer sought to discover attitudes on the marriage and sexual relationship, links between menstruation and sexual desire, and similar data that had never been studied.

The bureau quickly became a study center for many visiting doctors, social workers, and clergymen. The facts about the first eighteen hundred women given contraceptive help formed the basis of an important report to the Midwestern States Birth Control Conference in October 1923.

The Chicago Birth Control League now decided to open its own clinic and applied for a license to the health commissioner. When he rejected it, the league went to court and won a decision forcing the city to grant a license.

At the end of the second year, Margaret enlarged the bureau's services by enlisting a pool of physicians. Each volunteered a few hours' free time a week. She replaced the first medical director with the more experienced obstetrician-gynecologist Dr. Hannah Stone, who took the post without salary.

Dr. Stone was on the staff of a major hospital in New York. When she told the director she was going to serve the clinic, he said, "No doctor at this hospital can be associated with birth control." That night she resigned from the hospital.

The risk Dr. Stone took was shown again when her application for membership in the New York County Medical Society was "buried"—and not accepted until years later, after birth control had become "respectable."

Hannah Stone was perfectly fitted for this new role not only by her courage and medical skill but, as Margaret later said, "through her infinite patience, her understanding of human frailties, her sympathy and her gentleness." She became one of the most beloved leaders of the movement.

The number of patients increased so rapidly that Margaret moved the clinic to larger quarters at 46 West Fifteenth Street. Here there were individual consultation rooms, an examination room, a treatment room, even a playroom for children. In 1925 there were 1,655 patients; by 1929 the number had risen to 9,737—and each of these averaged about three visits. The figures also showed that despite the opposition of the church, as many Catholic patients—26 percent—came to the clinic as their rough proportion of the general population. Protestants made up 38 percent; Jews, 32 percent.

So many doctors wrote the bureau for information on its work and methods that in 1925 one session of the International Birth Control Conference in New York was devoted to Dr. Stone's report. A thousand doctors crowded the hall, which could not hold them all. A second session had to be arranged.

Dr. Stone reported that the most effective contraceptive method had proved to be the diaphragm when fitted carefully by the physician and used along with a chemical jelly. So far the failure rate of this method had been only 4 percent. The researchers were not completely satisfied with the chemical jelly, which Margaret imported from Germany. It was also quite expensive, and they were now developing new jellies.

That International Birth Control Conference was a landmark. Eight hundred delegates came from eighteen countries, including China, India, Rumania, and Soviet Russia. Twenty-four colleges were represented, and seventy-nine religious and sociological institutions.

For the first time, a leader of the American Medical Association, ex-president Dr. William A.

Pusey, supported birth control wholeheartedly. He said, "Women have a right to know how they can intelligently—not crudely and dangerously—control their sexual lives."

At the end, delegates from seven nations met to form the first international birth control organization. Margaret was unanimously elected president, but insisted that a scientist of international reputation should take the post, and Dr. C. C. Little was chosen. The central office was opened in London—the forerunner of today's International Planned Parenthood Federation with branches throughout the world.

After the 1925 conference the medical profession gradually gave more and more support to birth control. Now Margaret set out to get the backing of prominent figures in the field, and particularly of Dr. Robert L. Dickinson, recognized as the dean of American gynecologists. He was the head of the National Committee on Maternal Health, and winning their endorsement would be the final triumph.

At first Dr. Dickinson believed that birth control clinics should be attached to major hospitals. But he discovered that hospitals and their staffs were still too timid. Then he wanted more prominent doctors on the bureau's board and complete separation from the campaigning activities of the Birth Control League.

He was finally won over by Dr. Stone's bureau report in 1928, based on a three-year study of eleven hundred cases. It was so impressive a study that Dickinson himself had it published in a major medical journal and called it "a pioneer contribution."

In 1929 Margaret separated the bureau completely from the Birth Control League, and the next year Dr. Dickinson threw his full prestige behind it by joining the board. Each year new clinics had been added—in Detroit, Cleveland, Philadelphia, and on across the country to San Francisco and Los Angeles. By 1930 there were fifty-five clinics in twenty-three cities, an almost miraculous outcome of Margaret's dream that had started in the Brownsville slum fourteen years earlier.

16. CLINICS ACROSS THE COUNTRY

From the handful of devoted followers meeting in Margaret's apartment, the movement had now grown to a nation-wide organization. Local chapters of the Birth Control League had sprung up across the country. Yet, just at this time of rapid progress, there was serious trouble inside the league itself.

President from the start, Margaret had shown little interest in the details of organization. That burden had been carried by the board of directors. Gradually the board added to itself more and more women from national organizations who were used to careful controls kept tightly in the hands of an executive group. These women—the "conservatives"—could not understand Margaret's highly personal and often impulsive style of leadership.

From its first days Margaret had carried the movement on faith and inspiration. If a pamphlet had to be printed, a magazine published, a meeting held, she would act instantly and worry about paying for it later. Somehow the money was always found.

But the conservatives wanted every penny planned and accounted for. They were not used to personal leadership. Margaret was president, yes, but they expected her nevertheless to check every decision, big or little, with the whole board.

Sometimes it got ridiculous. Margaret found, for example, that the subscriptions to the *Birth Control Review* had fallen off sharply because the office had failed to send out renewal notices. She told the bookkeeper to spend the twenty dollars needed for an immediate mailing. "But I can't," the bookkeeper said. "Any expenditure over five dollars has to wait for approval at the next board meeting!"

The conservatives even cut into Margaret's authority as editor of the *Review*. They appointed a board of four to which she had to report for approval of every decision.

Then when she went off to Europe to plan the next population conference, the conservatives used her absence to cut her down still further. They refused to reelect to the board her old associate

Anne Kennedy, who had served as Margaret's chief lieutenant for the last eight years.

The old fighting spirit of the league was fast disappearing. Decay had set in. The conservatives wanted only to be safe, to do the accepted thing. To them the gains the movement had made were enough. Why take risks or invite danger?

These were women of high social position. They wanted the movement to be acceptable to their own class. But Margaret, the radical, had built the movement by challenging law and social custom. And in the beginning it had been only the radicals who had the vision and courage to sustain her.

The conservatives saw it differently. In their eyes the movement had outgrown Margaret. The old pioneers weren't needed any longer. They wanted to put leadership in the hands of women of wealth and leisure who took birth control as another chore of charity or welfare work.

But for Margaret birth control was more than routine and red tape. It was not something you tended to between tea parties. It was the first thing she thought about each day upon waking, and the last thing with her when sleep came.

By 1929 the split in the league had become so deep that Margaret decided to resign. Five of her oldest associates left with her. Mr. Slee also gave up the position of treasurer. The only official post Margaret still held was the directorship of the Clinical Research Bureau. This would always remain the heart of her work.

But even here, trouble swamped Margaret

again. On March 29, 1929, a woman calling herself Mrs. Tierney came to the bureau and was
examined by one of the staff physicians who found
several pelvic disorders. She was given a contraceptive because the doctor felt she should not
have another child too soon after the last one.

Mrs. Tierney returned on April 15—this time
using her real name, Policewoman Anna K. Mc-
Namara, and bringing with her a squad of seven
police officers.

Leading the raid was the chief of the Policewoman's Bureau, Mrs. Mary Sullivan. She had already arrested Dr. Stone, another doctor, and
three nurses by the time Margaret, who had been
called at her apartment, rushed down to the
clinic.

Police were trying to bully fifteen badly frightened patients into giving their names. Margaret
quietly assured the women that they need not
give their names and would not be arrested. One
detective tried to enter the room where a patient
was being examined. Dr. Stone stood in the doorway, refusing to let him pass.

The police were carting away everything in
sight—books, diagrams, contraceptive material.
Then Margaret saw Patrolwoman McNamara
starting to remove case histories of patients from
the files. It was a shocking violation of medical
ethics. These records contained patients' most personal statements and were considered a sacred
trust by the doctors. Not even the nurses had ac-
cess to them.

"You cannot touch those records!" Margaret

told Mrs. Sullivan. Scornfully Mrs. Sullivan produced a search warrant signed by Chief Magistrate McAdoo.

Margaret immediately phoned Dr. Dickinson at the Academy of Medicine. Horrified by this violation of ethics, Dickinson called Morris Ernst, a distinguished lawyer who had long been prominent in civil rights cases.

The police now took the doctors and nurses off to the station house where they were released on bail. Margaret and Mr. Ernst agreed the point of attack should be the police seizure of the patients' records. What authority do you have to do this? Ernst demanded of the police.

Magistrate McAdoo admitted his mistake when he said he had automatically signed the search warrant among the dozens placed on his desk each morning. He had the police bring him the records and locked them in his personal safe. The New York press attacked this action. "If the police can seize doctors' files without a specific warrant and paw over them in search of possible evidence, the privileged relation of doctor and client ceases to exist," said the *Herald Tribune*. "The possibilities of abuse, including blackmail, are virtually unlimited."

The medical profession, also, fought back. The Academy of Medicine called the raid a menace to "the freedom of the medical profession." When the trial opened on April 19 before Magistrate Rosenbluth, the academy had lined up some of the most important physicians in New York City to testify. From the records of medical examination by bureau physicians, Ernst easily proved that Policewoman McNamara's physical condition called for contraceptive help under the meaning of the 1918 Crane decision. All the academy's medical experts supported this conclusion.

But Ernst hoped to enlarge the Crane decision. He and Margaret wanted to establish that a birth control clinic is essential to public health. They wanted the law to agree that the spacing of children is vital to a mother's health.

Asked if too many children close together were a danger, Dr. Louis I. Harris, former New York City Commissioner of Health, told the court, "It aggravates and may, in fact, precipitate invalidism." Dr. Foster Kennedy added, "Recuperation for the mother depends upon proper spacing."

Such expert statements made the outcome of the trial almost certain. Magistrate Rosenbluth's decision completely supported the bureau. He made it clear that birth control clinics are "an important public health measure and a valuable aid in the conservation of family health," as Dr. Stone summed it up.

As a result, in the next eight years the number of clinics in the United States and Canada rose from 55 to 374. In New York the number of patients grew so rapidly that in 1930 Mr. Slee bought a handsome redbrick mansion at 17 West Sixteenth Street as the new home for the bureau.

All this while, Margaret had been giving more and more attention to the world movement. By

1926 Mussolini was already asking Italian mothers to produce more children, so that a new Italian empire could spread through the Mediterranean. The Japanese warlords demanded a ten-million population increase to support the army soon to invade Manchuria. And German nationalists were calling on Germany to expand from sixty-six to ninety millions.

In Margaret's eyes, the danger of population explosion and war was great. She wanted the crisis to be brought before the League of Nations. In a dramatic move she organized a World Population Conference that met in Geneva in 1927. It placed the issue right at the door of the League of Nations.

To continue her study of the international problem at close range, Margaret made many more trips abroad. In 1934 she visited the Soviet Union, taking Grant (about to enter his final year at Cornell Medical School) and a small party with her. She wanted to see the first Socialist state that had proclaimed it meant to emancipate women. Besides, she had heard that a Russian scientist had developed an injection, a "spermatoxin," that could prevent a woman from having a child for a period of weeks or even months.

Russia turned out to be full of contradictions. To give its women the right of free choice in deciding whether or not to become a mother, the government had made abortions legal. These were done at good hospitals by expert doctors at almost no cost.

But where were the birth control clinics? Why weren't women taught contraception to spare them repeated abortions? At hospital after hospital Margaret saw consultation rooms on birth control only to find they were rarely used and the contraceptive supplies outdated and untouched.

When Margaret finally reached one of the leading government officials and asked him whether Russia had a population policy, he told her curtly that no policy was needed. Russia, he insisted, was short of workers. Also Margaret discovered the government, already fearing the threat of Hitler's Germany, now wanted a higher birth rate. Thus the demands of history had changed what had seemed like a promising blueprint for birth control.

She was equally disappointed in her search for the birth control injection. She talked to the researcher in Leningrad who had developed it, but the government had halted all experiments. He did, however, allow her to take the formula home. When tested for two years at the University of Pennsylvania, it showed uncertain results. But she would not give up her dream of a long-lasting chemical contraceptive.

The next year she was in India. Its problem was overwhelming. The birth rate had shot up with frightening speed, yet millions of infants died before their first birthday. The maternal death rate was six times that of Britain. The new generation of Indian leaders supported birth control. But how could they reach the endless masses, the millions of peasants and workers cut off from modern methods by inability to read, by ignorance and superstition?

Margaret spoke all over the vast country at the invitation of the All-India Women's Conference. She met enthusiastic audiences at every stop— Bombay University, Calcutta, Allahabad, Madras, Malabar. The impact of her ten-thousand-mile tour was astounding: forty-five medical societies planned birth control programs; fifty birth control information centers were set up in hospitals and clinics.

Yet her trip knew one failure—the outcome of her visit to Mahatma Gandhi, the revered and mystic symbol of Indian independence. She arrived at Wardha, a tiny village in central India, and was taken to Gandhi's home in a two-wheel covered cart, drawn by a cream-colored bullock. Gandhi rose to greet her, smiling. "Around him and a part of him," Margaret wrote, "was a luminous aura . . . an unusual light that shines through the flesh."

They talked frankly, but could not agree. Although Gandhi favored small families, his solution was not birth control by mechanical or chemical means but the use of almost saintlike self-control, which he himself, but few others on earth, had mastered. Why could not women learn to say no to their husbands? he asked. "Why should people not be taught that it is immoral to have more than three or four children and that after they have had that number they should live separately?"

Margaret argued that this solution was impractical for most people. It would lead to divorce. And almost every psychiatrist said that such rigid self-control could be dangerous to mental health and family harmony. But Gandhi was convinced that man's spiritual nature could learn to rise above the needs of the body. He would not be budged.

From India Margaret circled through the Far East—Burma, Malaya, Hong Kong, China, the Philippines. In the midst of this frantic schedule, she was taken ill with a gall bladder attack. She put off the operation until she could reach home. She insisted on going on to Tokyo, although the militarists now in power were suppressing and even jailing advocates of birth control. Still, Margaret managed to hold a press conference. In Honolulu she was sick again, but with a doctor's help she finished her eight lectures.

Together with the World Population Conference, this 1935 trip advanced the growing international movement. At a dinner shortly after Margaret's return, the novelist Pearl Buck said of her: "She has started the fire of a great freedom. . . . No cause ever fought has been fought against more stupid, blind social prejudice. . . . She has been a pioneer in a great scientific and humane movement. . . . It is sure that her name will go down in history."

17. THE DOCTOR'S BILL

At the same time Margaret was building the international movement, she was marshaling her forces for an all-out attack on the last big barrier to birth control. It was the hated Comstock law.

This was the law under which Margaret had first been indicted for the *Woman Rebel* and *Family Limitation*. It was the law that struck fear into physicians, blocking them from using the mails to send or secure contraceptive information or supplies. It was the law that hampered birth control courses in medical schools. It was the law that limited scientific research. It was the law that made public announcements of birth control clinics illegal.

For almost sixty years the Comstock law had shackled the lives of American women. Now Margaret was sure the time had come to replace it with a new federal law—the "Doctor's Bill" as she called it. It would open up the mails to birth control information and materials sent by doctors, hospitals, or druggists for the care of patients.

To get the new bill through Congress, Margaret organized the National Committee for Federal Legislation for Birth Control. Its task was gigantic: to rally every woman in America behind the bill. Margaret realized the obstacles against passage. But even if the bill failed, the educational rewards of reaching millions of new women and organizations would be great. Her success can be judged by the fact that the committee eventually got the support of a thousand organizations, speaking for twenty million women.

Margaret set up committee headquarters in the nation's capital late in 1929. The Washington work was directed by Mrs. Thomas Hepburn, Mrs. Alexander Dick, and Mrs. Hazel Moore. The country was divided into three regions, each with its chairman and officers.

It was at the local level that the real work was done. One typical woman worker in Tacoma secured thirty-three statements of support for the bill from women's organizations, and almost twenty-five hundred individual signatures.

Margaret's aim was to get the support of almost every major national organization. Sometimes it took years of carefully wooing local chapters before the pressure was built high enough to win over the national body.

Religious groups were a prime target. One of the first to support the bill was the American Unitarian Association. It was followed by the Presbyterians, the Universalists, and the Central Conference of American Rabbis. Perhaps most important was the 1931 decision of the Federal Council of Churches of Christ in America, a parent body including twenty-three million Protestant members. It called for the repeal of all federal and state legislation that interfered with birth control information.

In Washington, Margaret and the staff worked tirelessly. They buttonholed members of Congress, spent weeks on end roaming the Senate and House office buildings to pin down elusive members for their endorsement. To introduce the bill in the Senate, Margaret secured a noted Republican, Frederick Gillett of Massachusetts. Guiding the bill through the tangle of Congressional procedure, he sent it to the Judiciary Committee whose chairman, Senator George Norris, was favorable to it. Norris appointed a subcommitee of three for hearings on February 13, 1931.

On that morning Margaret stood before the committee and quietly read part of the impressive list of the bill's national supporters. She wore a simple black dress with turtleneck collar. "I still cannot believe this is *the* Mrs. Sanger," one reporter wrote. "Her face, sober or smiling, has a kind of wistful quality, and her lovely auburn hair turns up in a soft natural roll at the back of her neck. How anyone could bear to commit her to jail for even an hour I can't imagine."

Margaret had brought authorities from many fields to testify—ministers, doctors, economists, spokesmen for leading women's groups, such as the Junior League. Since the adoption of the Comstock law, she told the committee, an estimated fifteen million infants had died in their first year of life. Many could have been living today, she said, if proper spacing of births had permitted their mothers to regain their strength after previous pregnancies. "We want children to be conceived in love, born of parents' conscious desire, and born into the world with healthy and sound bodies and minds," she concluded.

Then the forces opposing the bill testified— the Society for the Suppression of Vice, the Purity League, the Patriotic Society, and the Roman Catholic spokesmen.

"We are not imposing any legislation on the Catholics," Margaret said in reply. "They have a perfect right to use the method of self-control if they wish; but we do believe that we have just as much right under the Constitution to enjoy health, peace, and the right to pursuit of happiness as we see it."

The two senators attending the hearing listened to both sides. One voted against the bill, the other for it. The third, who had not come in for even a minute of the testimony, killed the bill with his negative vote.

Almost two years of backbreaking work seemed to have been lost that morning. But before the day was over, Margaret had given orders to start the drive for reintroduction of the bill at the next session. "Life has taught me one supreme lesson," she said. "This is that we must—if we are really to *live* at all—put our convictions into action."

The new campaign was based upon the most effective of all political pressures—letters from women written directly to their congressmen, urging them to support the Doctor's Bill. On her visits to the offices of congressmen, Margaret found these letters piled on their desks. Walking through the corridors one day, she met a senator who pulled from his pocket the letter of a woman describing the effect of too many children on her health and family. "I've never read anything so awful," he said. He introduced himself as Senator Henry D. Hatfield of West Virginia. Later he agreed to become a sponsor of the bill.

As national support for the bill increased, so did the frantic attacks of the opposition. After a number of prominent women representing important organizations testified for the bill at the next hearing, Father Charles E. Coughlin, a Roman Catholic priest from Detroit, Michigan, who ran a popular network radio program, snapped: "All this bill means is 'How to fornicate and not get caught.'"

There was shocked silence in the hearing room, then a buzz of angry voices. Some of the

women rose in their seats as if to attack Coughlin, but Margaret motioned them back. "Here
were these fine decent women, standing for all
that was best in motherhood, and they had practically been told to their faces that they were
prostitutes!"

In 1934 the Doctor's Bill was again introduced.
This time the way was prepared by a national
campaign in which thirty speakers gave 826 lectures in a year. The bill received more congressional backing than ever, and for the first time
was reported out of committee to the full Senate.
On the last day of the session there were two
hundred bills ahead of it. Margaret and her associates waited tensely in the gallery as one bill
after another came up—then the Doctor's Bill.
Miraculously it passed quickly, not a single voice
raised against it.

There was one more hurdle, a twenty-four-
hour time limit for any senator to ask for unani-
mous consent to recall the bill. Twenty minutes
later, Senator Pat McCarran, a prominent Roman Catholic, rushed to the floor and asked for
recall. The bill was referred back to the committee—which killed it. Its supporters were bitterly
disappointed.

The next year, 1935, marked the twenty-first
anniversary of the birth control movement. The
officers of the national committee decided to celebrate the occasion with a "Coming-of-Age Dinner." It would be a closing of the ranks, too, behind the new drive for the Doctor's Bill. The

dinner was sold out with twelve hundred reservations. A precedent was set when CBS agreed to carry the speeches. Amelia Earhart, Pearl Buck, and Dorothy Thompson spoke in the first network radio discussion of birth control.

It was just a few days before the dinner when the Doctor's Bill was again killed in committee. Margaret's associates were plunged into gloom, many wanting to postpone the dinner. Margaret refused. She insisted it must be the kickoff for a new legislative campaign.

Her unquenchable spirit brought new allies into the movement. The latest was Congressman Percy L. Gassaway of Oklahoma, who introduced the bill at the next session. He had fathered fourteen children, seven of whom had died, and he had lost his first wife in childbirth. "So I am convinced if birth control information had been available, as it will be if my bill is passed," he said, "our children would have been stronger and my wife would have survived."

But the bill failed again—and again and again. In fact, Margaret and the national committee never succeeded in repealing the old Comstock law. They were forced to turn instead to a different avenue of attack: the courts.

The long campaign for the Doctor's Bill had not been useless. It woke millions to the need for reform. And now, knowing they had popular support, the timid medical profession began to give their backing to birth control. In 1931 the New York Academy of Medicine demanded that all federal and state laws give doctors complete freedom to impart contraceptive information. As more and more scientific bodies favored birth control, public opinion in turn responded with even greater support. By 1935 a *Fortune* magazine survey showed that two out of three Americans wanted birth control information available to all.

18. CHALLENGE—AND VICTORY

Births go down when unemployment goes up. That is one of the symptoms of a depression. In the 1930s America was suffering the worst depression it had ever known. The birth rate dropped dramatically. The size of the average family shrank faster than in any decade before. Many couples said they wanted only two children because they feared they could never support more. Besides, who would want to bring children into a world that seemed to have no use for them?

By the third winter of the depression there were fourteen million unemployed—more than one out of every four workers. When Roosevelt's New

Deal government came into office that spring, it launched a big program of work relief. By 1935 twenty-two million people were on the federal relief rolls. Half the nation's births were in families on relief, struggling to survive on less than a thousand dollars a year.

Margaret saw the terrible consequences—fear, cold, hunger. It had made its mark on the faces of the people she met on her tours of the country. And on her desk in New York, mounting higher and higher, were stacks of requests for birth control help from relief officials and public health workers. Until the depression's end was in sight, they believed population had to be kept as low as possible. And Margaret agreed. The depression, she said in a speech, "will pass on to the coming generations a greater debt than the millions spent to feed the needy if relief officials continue to ignore birth control."

She knew why they ignored it. They were scared, scared by federal and local laws. She was trying to change the laws, but action in the legislatures was agonizingly slow. It was time for action on another front, she decided. The courts seemed to be more sensitive to social change than the lawmakers.

Since Judge Crane's 1918 decision, she had won continued victories in the courts. Now she and her lawyer, Morris Ernst, decided to attack again in what was to become one of the most important cases of the movement, the "One Package" case.

It started when Margaret asked that samples

of a new Japanese pessary be sent to her New York office. When the package arrived, it was seized by the collector of customs under the Comstock law.

Here was a chance to challenge the law because it interfered with the free flow of information within the medical profession. Margaret arranged to have another package sent, this time by a Japanese doctor directly to Dr. Hannah Stone. Again customs agents seized it, and Dr. Stone took her claim to court, with Mr. Ernst as her lawyer. The case came to trial in December 1935.

Ernst argued that the government could not prevent contraception from being mailed to a physician, even from a foreign country, when it would be used to safeguard the life and health of mothers and children. Medical experts came into court to support the significant role of birth control in maternal health.

Impressed by the testimony, the court upheld this position, and ordered the Collector of Customs to deliver the package to Dr. Stone. The government appealed to a higher court, and on November 10, 1936, Judge Augustus N. Hand upheld the previous decision.

Ernst hailed it as both "a legal triumph" and "a medical triumph." But Margaret delayed her celebration until the government decided whether to appeal to the United States Supreme Court. In January 1937 the United States Attorney General announced the government would not challenge the ruling. The birth control movement had won!

The decision not only gave physicians the right to import contraceptive materials. It went much further. It opened up the mails at home to all materials and literature to and from doctors and other qualified persons. As Dr. Stone wrote, the decision "once and for all established contraception as a recognized part of medical practice and removed the last legal barriers to the dissemination of contraceptive knowledge."

Margaret proudly called it "the close of one epoch and the dawn of another."

A few months later came equally dramatic news. All through the years, although the leading medical groups had ignored or even insulted her, Margaret had stuck to her belief that contraception must be taught and handled by doctors. At last, "smashing a twenty-five year taboo," as one paper put it, the American Medical Association decided at its 1937 meeting to support birth control and public education in the field. When Margaret, who was at her country home, saw the headlines in the paper, she was so excited that she tripped and fell downstairs.

The One Package case made it possible for Margaret to launch a daring project she had long been developing in her mind. The rich had few problems about getting the means of birth control. They had a head start in adopting it. The years of public discussion had overcome resistance to its use. Early in the depression a poll of the readers of a farm magazine showed two to one in favor of having advice on birth control available. Gas stations had begun to sell contraceptives, and the Sears Roebuck catalogue was now offering them. But the poorest women, especially those who lived in rural areas far from the big cities, had never been reached by birth control clinics.

The one agency that touched their lives was the state public health service. Up to now, the Comstock law had stopped the flow of information to these doctors. With this obstacle removed, why couldn't birth control become a state service? Why couldn't mothers go to state health clinics for contraception as easily as for typhoid shots?

Margaret took the field organization of the National Committee and moved it into the Clinical Research Bureau, making it the new Education Department. Its first target was the worst poverty region in the country—the South. Her chief ally was Dr. George N. Cooper of the North Carolina Board of Health. He had long been distressed by the high death rate of infants in his state. He was convinced the spacing of children through contraception would cut down these deaths.

In 1937 he established the first birth control services at state clinics. Within a year he had enlarged the program to the point where no family was more than fifty miles from contraceptive help.

Florida, Virginia, and seven more states soon

followed the lead of Dr. Cooper in North Carolina. In 1939 Margaret shifted the focus of her
Education Department to the next target—the
tragic dustbowl of the Southwest where small
farmers had been crippled by a long dry spell
coming on top of the depression.

Poverty-stricken farmers, driven from their
land by dust storms, disease, and inability to pay
their bank loans, were moving westward. Their
eyes were on the rich valleys of California where
they hoped life would be better. Now their
shacks, windowless, without water or toilets,
pocked California's fields and orchards. Out-
breaks of disease were common, medical care
rare. Girls married as young as thirteen and often
had ten children before they were thirty.

Margaret's field workers surveyed the migrant
camps. The women they talked to knew almost
nothing about contraception and little more
about the functions of their own bodies. One
grandmother, discussing her daughter Sara, said,
"I've had thirteen myself. Got fifty-three grandchildren. If Sara is goin' to work from kin-see to
cain't-see every day, she ought to stop havin' kids
a spell."

Margaret went out to help her field workers.
She brought them an efficient plan for birth control programs in all the camps as well as a large
supply of contraceptives and teaching materials.
Soon the camp bulletin boards began to show
new announcements:

OLD TIME DANCE TONIGHT
TYPHOID VACCINATION THURSDAY
BIRTH CONTROL CLINIC FRIDAY

All meetings were voluntary, but the mothers were soon calling ones of their own. At one local school the teacher announced meetings by pinning slips to the clothing of the children. The federal agencies that ran these camps gave their full support. By 1940 birth control services were operating in twenty-five camps in California and Arizona.

The rapid growth of clinics made the existence of two separate organizations—Margaret's new Education Department and the old Birth Control League—more difficult. There were almost six hundred clinics now; some joined to one, some to the other, and a few to both. The professional fund raisers, who were studying the problems of both organizations, insisted there must be a merger of the two.

Margaret did not oppose it. She felt the pioneering days of the American movement were almost over. After long discussion a merger was completed in 1939. The name of the new organization—Planned Parenthood Federation of America—showed how times had changed.

The struggle to break the chains of what Margaret called "an enslaved motherhood" had given way to a new era. PPF was concerned with the planning of total family life, including marriage counseling and psychological guidance, to achieve health and happiness.

Margaret was elected honorary chairman of the new PPF, and a prominent physician, Dr. Richard N. Pierson, was chosen president. All functions of the two old organizations were unified into PPF except the Clinical Research Bureau, whose building Mr. Slee had given Margaret and which she insisted must remain her personal responsibility.

From then on, Margaret would spend only a small part of her time on the national movement. She was ready to concentrate on the world movement, on what someone called her "plans for the planet."

Marking the change, Professor Norman Himes of Colgate University, author of a major population study, summed up Margaret's effect on the last twenty-five years: "No reformer in human history—and I weigh my words well—no reformer has lived to see the things she stood for so completely brought about."

19. AROUND THE WORLD

Margaret's strength would be tested in many hard and lonely hours now. Within a few years, all the men she had loved most would be gone. Her father, Michael Higgins, had died in 1926 at the age of eighty-four. She had given him her Cape Cod house for the last years of his life. He had tramped into town every day to buy his groceries, delivered his daily speech on politics to the grocer, and then settled down at home with his favorite books and the tonic of his old age, local dandelion wine.

After a stroke he lingered awhile and then died. He was buried in the Corning cemetery next to the wife he adored. Hundreds of stone angels that he had carved looked on from the Catholic cemetery nearby. He remained nonreligious to the end, asking that there be no minister or prayers at his grave.

Her father had been the first to make Margaret believe that human beings had the power to shape their own lives, and she recognized her debt to him. Once when discussing the title for her autobiography, she suggested with a smile, "Men I Have Loved." Then she added seriously, "Beginning, of course, with my father."

The next to go was Havelock Ellis. On his eightieth birthday in 1939, Margaret sailed to England to spend it with him. She brought with her a gift from all his friends in America. "Havelock," she said, "one wanted to give you peach trees for your garden, another a new library, a third a new phonograph. But I couldn't carry these and all the other gifts with me." Quietly she placed a large envelope of money in his pocket.

He smiled gently. "Margaret, you are the most wonderful and practical of women."

It was only a few weeks after she left that Ellis came down with a fever and died. He had been a powerful influence in her life and on the world's thinking. His books on the relations between the sexes had lit up the dark corners of the mind.

Two years later, Dr. Hannah Stone was gone, the victim of a heart attack at the age of forty-

seven. It was not long after—just before Christmas 1941—that Margaret's husband was stricken.
They had bought a home in Tucson, Arizona, in
the lovely foothills at the edge of the city. He
had fallen—possibly it was a light stroke—but
recovered enough to go to Willow Lake that
spring. Then he suffered a severe stroke that left
him partially paralyzed. They returned to Tucson so that he could enjoy the sun. Margaret
gave up all speeches and other work to be with
him constantly. She read to him every afternoon.
Once he said, "I can remember every detail of
that first lunch together, every place we went,
everything we did. Only since I first saw you do
I remember anything."

He died in June 1942, and Stuart who was in
the army and Grant in the navy were able to fly
back and sit beside Margaret at the funeral service. Speaking of him, an old friend, Dorothy
Brush, said, "You doubtless sent St. Peter a tele-
gram saying you'd be at the gate at such and
such a time and to be sure to have it open for
you. You reserved the best suite on the most comfortable heavenly cloud. If everything wasn't as
you thought it ought to be, you would be sure to
shout in an outraged tone, 'Where's Margaret?'
Then you'd remember, dear Noah, and heaven
wouldn't be heaven after all."

The war had made Margaret's loneliness even
deeper. Grant was in the Pacific, his ship en-
gaged in heavy action. Stuart served in Europe
and was eventually invalided back to England.

Both sons had married, and it was fortunate in those years that she could busy herself with her grandchildren. Stuart's first child was named after Margaret; the second was named Nancy. Grant's first son was named Michael after his grandfather.

Stuart's children called her "Mimi." Grant's had their own pet name for her, "Domah," which is similar to the Chinese expression for "second mother." But when they were shouting at her to join in a game, she was "Dommie," or "Dom."

After the war Margaret sold the house at Willow Lake and made Tucson her permanent home. She built a new house, working on the plans with the architect and decorating it herself. It was on one level, with the rooms radiating from the entrance hall. From the air it looked like a fan shimmering in the bright desert sun.

Stuart's family lived in the house next door. At Christmastime she always went to Mt. Kisco, New York, to be with Grant and his family. They had a handsome house in the hills. Margaret, who had become a good painter, did a mural in the children's dining room, each of the six light-hearted scenes honoring one of the grandchildren. She seemed to be able to reach children as easily as she did some of the greatest men of her time. She was always, as Hugh de Sélincourt said, "a delicious blend of great queen and shy little girl."

In those few years after World War II, some of

Margaret's closest friends thought she had cut herself off from the birth control movement. But they were wrong. She had not retired for good. Past sixty now, she was taking a rest she had earned. Why shouldn't she be Tucson's leading socialite for a while? Why shouldn't she enjoy the honors due a great crusader?

What even her closest friends didn't know was that this was a period of change. Retirement? Old age? None of the usual limits of life affected her. She was simply storing up power for a new burst of activity.

Her energy seemed endless. After a busy day she thought nothing of driving fifty miles to a dinner party and staying up till two in the morning. When Dorothy Brush visited Tucson, she and Margaret went to meetings and dinner parties nine nights in a row. On the tenth, Mrs. Brush insisted on going to bed early. "Are you sick?" Margaret asked. Just tired, her guest explained. But Margaret called the doctor anyway. She couldn't believe that anyone would give up a good dinner party because she was a little worn.

Margaret had always ignored the limits of her own physical condition. Despite a heart attack just before she was to move into her new Tucson home, she called for the moving men as soon as she got out of the hospital. Mrs. Brush rushed out to take over, but Margaret wouldn't hear of it. She worked side by side with her friend, angry at the least suggestion that someone else do the work. "Don't pity her, pity the doctors!" Mrs. Brush said.

The wreckage of World War II had finally roused many nations to the necessity for population control, which Margaret had called for over twenty-five years ago. Germany's murderous assault on Europe and Japan's invasion of the Far East in their hunt for "living space" were frightening proof of the link between population and war.

Japan's problem was desperate. There had been almost sixty million people crowded into the tiny islands when Margaret visited in 1922. Now there were eighty million.

India's need was even worse. In the nineteen-thirties its population had increased by fifty million—equal to the total population of Britain.

When the first meeting of the International Planned Parenthood Federation was scheduled for India in November 1952, Margaret decided to visit Japan first. She wanted to aid its struggling birth control movement. But upon asking for a visa, she encountered unexpected difficulty. General Douglas MacArthur, Supreme Commander for the Allied Powers, based in Tokyo, turned down her request. In 1922 it had been Japanese militarists who had tried to stop her. Now it was an American.

What was the reason? Probably because an American book on population problems had just been taken out of circulation after protests by the Catholic Women's Club of Tokyo. Catholics made up only a tiny fraction of Japan's population, but the general seemed unwilling to offend anyone.

Backed by many national organizations, Mar-

garet carried her fight for a visa right to the
United States Secretary for Defense. Then Mac-
Arthur was removed from command during the
last stage of the Korean War, and Margaret quickly got her visa.

Her arrival in Japan was described by a startled army officer on the dock as "the closest thing
to a Hollywood opening I've ever seen out here."
At seven o'clock in the morning, when her boat
docked, her stateroom was filled with forty reporters, and a hundred more waited at the gang-
plank. The crowds applauding her on the streets
and the distinguished audiences who packed her
meeting halls were witness to a national outpour-
ing of affection.

In ten short days she mobilized the country
behind birth control. She helped draw up a five-
year birth control plan—clinics, teaching centers,
an education program, research. Sound trucks
rolled through Tokyo's streets crying, "Sanger
is here!"

When she arrived in India for the conference,
it was a new kind of triumph. For the first time
in any country, government policy supported
birth control. India had already set up hundreds
of clinics, and birth control was part of Prime
Minister Nehru's new Five-Year Plan.

At the final conference session, the delegates
of birth control organizations from six nations
agreed to unite in the International Planned
Parenthood Federation. Margaret and Lady Rama
Rau of India were elected honorary presidents.

Margaret stood on the platform, a tiny figure, almost frail in her simple black dress. Waves of applause rolled toward her. She had gone to jail nine times. She had worked a lifetime for this moment. It was almost thirty-eight years to the month since she had sailed from Montreal, an exile from her own country. Since then, she had won the fight in the United States.

Now she was winning it throughout the world.

20. POPULATION, PEACE, AND PLENTY

Although Margaret's health failed increasingly in the last six years of her life, she remained the dynamic center of the movement—at least through 1960. The Clinical Research Bureau in New York was always her first concern. To insure it would go on, she turned over the building on West Sixteenth Street to a board of directors. It was renamed in her honor the Margaret Sanger Research Bureau.

It has continued to grow at a great rate, handling some twenty thousand patients a year now. Its emphasis has shifted to education for marriage. It counsels young couples before marriage, not just in contraception, but in planning for children and the handling of family problems. It continues research for new and better contraceptives, and trains doctors from all over the world in birth control programs they can take back to their own lands. Since more women in middle- and upper-income groups now get contraceptive help from their personal physicians, the bureau has steadily expanded its services into the low-income districts of New York.

As part of this expansion, the bureau bought the building next door. But its most dramatic growth will come in the early 1970s. At that time it will join Columbia University's International Institute for the Study of Human Reproduction and move to new quarters being constructed as part of the Columbia Presbyterian Medical Center.

An important addition to its program will be the proposed clinic for voluntary sterilization. Many international leaders—such as India's Minister of Family Planning who calls this technique "the physical salvation of mankind"—are convinced that voluntary sterilization is the long-range solution for birth control. In families who have as many children as they want, either the husband or wife can have a small pair of tubes closed, so that the male sperm and the female egg cannot meet. This guarantees that no more children can be conceived.

The new sterilization clinic of the Sanger Bureau will not only provide surgical services.

Above all, it will develop research toward the goal of making male sterilization reversible. This means that a man could have another simple operation—the removal of a tiny clip is one method being studied—which would allow him to father another child. The benefits of such research are great. A man and wife who have decided that they wish no more children for five or ten years may change their minds, and the husband need only go to his doctor to have the clip removed.

Outside New York, birth control clinics have grown astonishingly in recent years. The Planned Parenthood Federation of America, with 154 affiliates, now has four hundred clinics and serves about 350,000 women each year. Hundreds of thousands of others get contraceptive help from hospitals and public health clinics. But the major target of PPF has now become a large group of about 5,000,000 American women who are almost never reached by birth control. They are in low-income families, and most of them live in cities. Although many are blacks, Puerto Ricans, and members of other minority groups in the urban ghettos, a surprisingly large number belong to white families in rural areas. With all the progress the movement has made, it now faces its greatest challenge—the fact that one out of five American women of childbearing age still need protection against unwanted pregnancies.

Perhaps the most important symbol of growth is the International Planned Parenthood Federation. At its founding in 1952 it had a tiny office in London and a staff of one part-time assistant. By 1966 it had offices all over the world and gave contraceptive services in fifty-four countries on a budget of well over two million dollars.

Although Margaret's health limited her work for the International, she was able to raise crucial funds. Soon she was aided by Hugh Moore, a retired corporation president, who devoted all his time to the population movement. Moore was determined to put a solid financial base under IPPF. He not only paid for some of its staff and offices but in 1960 launched an emergency campaign. Margaret's personal inspiration was essential to the meeting, and from her sickbed she wrote, "If humanly possible, if I have to crawl, I will be there." Her speech helped raise a hundred thousand dollars on the spot. In 1961 the campaign reached its peak when world leaders paid tribute to Margaret at a banquet in New York's Waldorf Astoria Hotel, and another hundred thousand dollars was contributed.

In the last year of Margaret's life, the search for a chemical contraceptive—"the pill"—dominated every moment. Since her Russian trip in 1934 she had been driven by the belief that the world movement could never succeed without a pill or injection—something far simpler than the diaphragm or other methods.

She hammered endlessly at scientists and shouted the urgency of this cause wherever she went. At last, in 1950, Dr. Abraham Stone, who had followed his late wife as director of the bureau, introduced her to the right scientist, Dr. Gregory Pincus, research head of the Foundation for Experimental Biology in Shrewsbury, Massachusetts.

With a research fund that Margaret collected and would constantly add to with help from her friends, the foundation started work in 1951. The scientists' objective was to use female sex hormones, a crucial part of the body's glandular system, to control the woman's monthly ovulation—the time when she releases an egg that must be fertilized by male sperm to start the process of birth.

By discovering how these hormones can be taken by pill over a period of twenty days each month, Pincus and his associates were able to stop the regular monthly egg from being released (it's simply reabsorbed into the body). If there is no free egg, there is no fertile period when a woman can have a child. Thus the "pill" stretches out the infertile period indefinitely—until the woman wants to have a child and stops taking the pill.

Once the pill was developed, researchers had to conduct years of tests on thousands of women before the United States government permitted its production and sale on doctor's prescription. The pill proved to give protection against pregnancy as long as the woman follows directions exactly. By the late 1960s, despite some reports of damage from the pill, about one out of every six women of childbearing age in the United States had adopted this method of contraception. For Margaret, her dream was coming true, and within her lifetime.

There would be one final victory in her long battle against legal barriers to birth control. Despite a series of challenges to state laws starting with Margaret's own Brownsville clinic, there were still some states where laws prohibiting clinics or a free flow of contraceptive information remained in force. The worst offender was Connecticut, and a group of Planned Parenthood officials there brought a test case that was finally decided by the Supreme Court in 1965.

The decision, which said that "privacy in the marital relation is fundamental and basic," was a sweeping triumph for birth control. It not only wiped out the Connecticut law, but the law of any other state that still limited the use of contraception.

The victory came barely in time for Margaret to enjoy it. She had been weakened by repeated heart attacks over the last ten years; more and more she was confined to her bed. Finally her condition worsened so much that she had to be placed in a Tucson nursing home. Friends and family came to see her constantly. She loved to talk with them about the movement and send challenging memos to New York or London, demanding instant action on some idea that had stirred her. But she was eighty-seven. Her heart could not hold out much longer, and she died peacefully on September 6, 1966. She was buried in the cemetery at Fishkill, New York, near her old Willow Lake home.

The next day a *New York Times* editorial called her "one of history's great rebels and a monumental figure of the first half of the twentieth century." Almost every newspaper, including Catholic papers that had once attacked her bitterly, paid tribute to Margaret Sanger as a heroic fighter whose ideas and impact on the world were of immeasurable value.

Today the world has caught up with the crucial necessity for population control. Many political leaders consider it second only to the threat of nuclear war as the key issue of our time. World population is now growing at a record speed of seventy million a year. The terrible prophecy is that at the current rate of increase the world may double in population by the year 2000. Yet less than 5 percent of the world's six hundred-odd million women in the fertile years are using modern contraceptives. What does this mean? To Dr. Harrison Brown, one of the nation's leading scientists, it means "catastrophe appears a near certainty."

Latin America, whose growth is faster than any other continent's, will almost triple its population in the next three decades. And less food is now produced and eaten there per capita than before World War II. India, kept from the edge of famine by wheat shipments from abroad, will add two hundred million more people by 1980.

With this tidal wave of population goes des

perate hunger. One half of the world's population and two thirds of its children go to bed hungry every night. General William H. Draper, Jr., head of a presidential study committee has said that "the stark fact is that if the population continues to increase faster than food production, hundreds of millions will starve in the next decade."

The United States has already added fifty million between 1950 and 1968, and our population may almost double by the year 2000. We may not face famine because of our highly mechanized food production. But the terrible overcrowding in the cities has already brought us the destructive problems of air and water pollution, traffic chaos, shortage of schools and houses, lack of parks and recreation space. The whole quality of American life is being badly damaged.

Almost everyone now realizes that Margaret Sanger's crusade for population control is the only way to enable living standards to improve substantially. International Planned Parenthood has already shown in many areas that populations can be kept in reasonable balance. In Hong Kong and Singapore, birth rates were cut almost 40 percent in ten years. Japan is the most remarkable example of all. After the government approved legalized abortion in qualified hospitals, along with contraception, the country cut its birth rate more than in half between 1947 and 1961.

The need has become so staggering that IPPF has been joined by new allies. First came the private organizations. The Population Council, headed by John D. Rockefeller III, has spent over thirty-five million dollars since 1952, The Ford Foundation many millions more.

But the money needed to spread birth control around the world goes far beyond private means. Hugh Moore's Campaign to Check the Population Explosion and the Population Crisis Committee in Washington soon realized that only vast help from the federal government could meet the crisis. With constant pressure on Congress, they were able to get the government to increase its population programs overseas to fifty million dollars in 1969. Family planning programs in the United States were given ten million dollars. Yet even these sums are only a tiny fraction of what it will take to meet the problem.

The message that Margaret Sanger stamped forever on this age was that human beings could consciously control the plan and purpose of their lives, and that out of this independence, they could raise society to a new level of dignity and beauty.

Within fifty years this message spread from her first publication, *Woman Rebel*, to almost every corner of the world. Margaret's fight went much deeper than education or votes for women. It reached the vital core of their lives—the right to control their own bodies.

As the leader of a world movement, she went even further. She made birth control an instrument of social progress, an instrument that may now help shape the future of nations.

The social revolution she brought about in her own country has been so sweeping in the space of a few years that many young mothers today take birth control as much for granted as if it were written into our Constitution.

H. G. Wells, Margaret's old friend, said of her:

> Alexander the Great changed a few boundaries and killed a few men. Both he and Napoleon were forced into fame by circumstances outside of themselves and by currents of the time, but Margaret Sanger made currents and circumstances. When the history of our civilization is written, it will be a biological history and Margaret Sanger will be its heroine.

Bibliography

The most important published sources on Margaret Sanger's life are her own writings, many of which have been quoted in this biography.

WORKS BY MARGARET SANGER

What Every Mother Should Know. New York: Eugenics Publishing Co., 1916.

The Case for Birth Control. New York: privately printed, 1917.

Woman and the New Race. New York: Brentano, 1920.

The Pivot of Civilization. New York: Brentano, 1922.

What Every Girl Should Know. New York: Eugenics Publishing Co., 1922.

Happiness in Marriage. New York: Brentano, 1926.

Motherhood in Bondage. New York: Brentano, 1928.

My Fight for Birth Control. New York: Farrar & Rinehart, 1931.

Margaret Sanger, An Autobiography. New York: Norton, 1938.

BOOKS ON THE BIRTH CONTROL AND POPULATION
MOVEMENTS

BEARD, MARY. *Women as a Force in History*. New York: Macmillan, 1946.

COOK, ROBERT C., and LECHT, JANE. *People!* Washington, D.C.: Columbia Books, 1968.

DAY, LINCOLN H., and ALICE T. *Too Many Americans*. Boston: Houghton Mifflin, 1964.

EHRLICH, PAUL R. *The Population Bomb*. New York: Ballantine, 1968.

FRYER, PETER. *The Birth Controllers*. New York: Stein & Day, 1966.

GUTTMACHER, ALAN, M.D., ed. *The Case for Legalized Abortion*. Berkeley: Diablo Press, 1967.

GUTTMACHER, ALAN, M.D., with Winfield Best and Frederick S. Jaffe. *Planning Your Family—The Complete Guide to Contraception and Fertility*. New York: Macmillan, 1965.

HAVEMANN, ERNEST, and editors of Time-Life Books. *Birth Control*. New York: Time-Life Books, 1967.

JOHNSON, ERIC W. *Love and Sex in Plain Language*. New York: Bantam (Pathfinder Edition), 1968.

LADER, LAWRENCE. *Abortion*. New York: Bobbs-Merrill, 1966.

LENICA, JAN, and SAUVY, ALFRED. *Population Explosion—Abundance or Famine*. New York: Dell (Visual Book No. 5), 1962.

NAISMITH, GRACE. *Private and Personal*. New York: David McKay, 1966.

NEUBARDT, SELIG, M.D. *A Concept of Contraception.* New York: Trident, 1967.

PADDOCK, WILLIAM and PAUL. *Famine 1975!* Boston: Little, Brown, 1967.

ROCK, JOHN, M.D. *The Time Has Come—A Catholic Doctor's Proposals to End the Battle Over Birth Control.* New York: Alfred A. Knopf, 1963.

VOGT, WILLIAM. *Road to Survival.* New York: Sloane, 1948.

WOOD, H. CURTIS, JR., M.D. *Sex Without Babies.* Philadelphia: Whitemore Publishing Co., 1967.

For current information in the population field, the following organizations distribute publications of their own:

Hugh Moore Fund (Campaign to End the Population Explosion), 60 East 42d Street, New York, N.Y.

International Planned Parenthood Federation, 51 East 42d Street, New York, N.Y.

Planned Parenthood—World Population, 515 Madison Avenue, New York, N.Y.

Population Council, 245 Park Avenue, New York, N.Y.

Population Crisis Committee, 1730 K Street NW, Washington, D.C.

Population Reference Bureau, 1755 Massachusetts Avenue NW, Washington, D.C.

Sex Information and Education Council of the U.S. (SIECUS), 1855 Broadway, New York, N.Y.

Index

more good reading in
THE LAUREL-LEAF LIBRARY

If you cannot obtain copies of these titles from your local bookseller, just
send the price (plus 25c per copy for handling and postage) to Dell Books,
Post Office Box 1000, Pinebrook, N. J. 07058.